NAME	DATE			

MW01291544

QUICK RECAP LIST

NAME	DATE	PAGE NO.	QUALITY RATING	VALUE RATING

BOURBON	

PRODUCER		DISTILLERY	
TYPE / GRADE		COUNTRY	
ALCOHOL %		REGION	
AGE		STILL TYPE	
PRICE		BOTTLE SIZE	

QUALITY RATING

1	2	3	4	5	6	7	8	9	10

VALUE FOR MONEY

1	2	3	4	5	6	7	8	9	10

COLOR METER

BLACK

DARK BROWN

MAHOGANY

BRICK

DARK AMBER

AMBER

GOLD

STRAW

CLEAR

FLAVOR WHEEL

BALANCE • HEAT / ABM _____ %
FINISH • FRESH FRUIT
BODY • DARK FRUIT
ESTERY • CITRUS FRUIT
SHARP / ACIDIC • DRIED FRUIT
ASTRINGENT • HERBAL / VEGETAL
ROASTED / WOODY • SPICES
MOLASSES • SWEET / CANDIED

FLAVOR NOTES

SMELL / SCENT

OTHER NOTES

BOURBON	

PRODUCER		DISTILLERY	
TYPE / GRADE		COUNTRY	
ALCOHOL %		REGION	
AGE		STILL TYPE	
PRICE		BOTTLE SIZE	

QUALITY RATING

1	2	3	4	5	6	7	8	9	10

VALUE FOR MONEY

1	2	3	4	5	6	7	8	9	10

COLOR METER

BLACK

DARK BROWN

MAHOGANY

BRICK

DARK AMBER

AMBER

GOLD

STRAW

CLEAR

FLAVOR WHEEL

HEAT / ABM _____ %

BALANCE
FINISH
BODY
ESTERY
SHARP / ACIDIC
ASTRINGENT
ROASTED / WOODY
MOLASSES
SWEET / CANDIED
SPICES
HERBAL / VEGETAL
DRIED FRUIT
CITRUS FRUIT
DARK FRUIT
FRESH FRUIT

FLAVOR NOTES

. . . .
. . . .
. . . .
. . . .
. . . .
. . . .
. . . .
. . . .
. . . .
. . . .

SMELL / SCENT

. . . .
. . . .
. . . .
. . . .
. . . .
. . . .
. . . .

OTHER NOTES

. . . .
. . . .
. . . .
. . . .
. . . .
. . . .

BOURBON	

PRODUCER		DISTILLERY	
TYPE / GRADE		COUNTRY	
ALCOHOL %		REGION	
AGE		STILL TYPE	
PRICE		BOTTLE SIZE	

QUALITY RATING

1	2	3	4	5	6	7	8	9	10

VALUE FOR MONEY

1	2	3	4	5	6	7	8	9	10

COLOR METER

BLACK

DARK BROWN

MAHOGANY

BRICK

DARK AMBER

AMBER

GOLD

STRAW

CLEAR

FLAVOR WHEEL

HEAT / ABM _____ %

BALANCE
FINISH
BODY
ESTERY
SHARP / ACIDIC
ASTRINGENT
ROASTED / WOODY
MOLASSES
SWEET / CANDIED
SPICES
HERBAL / VEGETAL
DRIED FRUIT
CITRUS FRUIT
DARK FRUIT
FRESH FRUIT

FLAVOR NOTES

....
....
....
....
....
....
....
....
....
....
....

SMELL / SCENT

....
....
....
....
....
....
....

OTHER NOTES

....
....
....
....
....
....
....

BOURBON	

PRODUCER		**DISTILLERY**	
TYPE / GRADE		**COUNTRY**	
ALCOHOL %		**REGION**	
AGE		**STILL TYPE**	
PRICE		**BOTTLE SIZE**	

QUALITY RATING

1	2	3	4	5	6	7	8	9	10

VALUE FOR MONEY

1	2	3	4	5	6	7	8	9	10

COLOR METER

BLACK

DARK BROWN

MAHOGANY

BRICK

DARK AMBER

AMBER

GOLD

STRAW

CLEAR

FLAVOR WHEEL

HEAT / ABM _____ %

BALANCE
FINISH
BODY
ESTERY
SHARP / ACIDIC
ASTRINGENT
ROASTED / WOODY
MOLASSES
SWEET / CANDIED
SPICES
HERBAL / VEGETAL
DRIED FRUIT
CITRUS FRUIT
DARK FRUIT
FRESH FRUIT

FLAVOR NOTES

....
....
....
....
....
....
....
....
....
....

SMELL / SCENT

....
....
....
....
....
....

OTHER NOTES

....
....
....
....
....
....

BOURBON	

PRODUCER		DISTILLERY	
TYPE / GRADE		COUNTRY	
ALCOHOL %		REGION	
AGE		STILL TYPE	
PRICE		BOTTLE SIZE	

QUALITY RATING

1	2	3	4	5	6	7	8	9	10

VALUE FOR MONEY

1	2	3	4	5	6	7	8	9	10

COLOR METER

BLACK

DARK BROWN

MAHOGANY

BRICK

DARK AMBER

AMBER

GOLD

STRAW

CLEAR

FLAVOR WHEEL

HEAT / ABM _____ %

BALANCE
FINISH
BODY
ESTERY
SHARP / ACIDIC
ASTRINGENT
ROASTED / WOODY
MOLASSES
SWEET / CANDIED
SPICES
HERBAL / VEGETAL
DRIED FRUIT
CITRUS FRUIT
DARK FRUIT
FRESH FRUIT

FLAVOR NOTES

....
....
....
....
....
....
....
....
....
....

SMELL / SCENT

....
....
....
....
....
....

OTHER NOTES

BOURBON	

PRODUCER		DISTILLERY	
TYPE / GRADE		COUNTRY	
ALCOHOL %		REGION	
AGE		STILL TYPE	
PRICE		BOTTLE SIZE	

QUALITY RATING

1	2	3	4	5	6	7	8	9	10

VALUE FOR MONEY

1	2	3	4	5	6	7	8	9	10

COLOR METER

BLACK

DARK BROWN

MAHOGANY

BRICK

DARK AMBER

AMBER

GOLD

STRAW

CLEAR

FLAVOR WHEEL

BALANCE   HEAT / ABM _____ %
FINISH
BODY
ESTERY
SHARP / ACIDIC
ASTRINGENT
ROASTED / WOODY
MOLASSES
SWEET / CANDIED
SPICES
HERBAL / VEGETAL
DRIED FRUIT
CITRUS FRUIT
DARK FRUIT
FRESH FRUIT

FLAVOR NOTES

....
....
....
....
....
....
....
....
....
....
....

SMELL / SCENT

....
....
....
....
....
....

OTHER NOTES

....
....
....
....
....
....

14

BOURBON	

PRODUCER		DISTILLERY	
TYPE / GRADE		COUNTRY	
ALCOHOL %		REGION	
AGE		STILL TYPE	
PRICE		BOTTLE SIZE	

QUALITY RATING

1	2	3	4	5	6	7	8	9	10

VALUE FOR MONEY

1	2	3	4	5	6	7	8	9	10

COLOR METER

BLACK

DARK BROWN

MAHOGANY

BRICK

DARK AMBER

AMBER

GOLD

STRAW

CLEAR

FLAVOR WHEEL

BALANCE   HEAT / ABM _____ %

FINISH

BODY

FRESH FRUIT

ESTERY

DARK FRUIT

SHARP / ACIDIC

CITRUS FRUIT

ASTRINGENT

DRIED FRUIT

ROASTED / WOODY

HERBAL / VEGETAL

MOLASSES

SPICES

SWEET / CANDIED

FLAVOR NOTES

. . . .
. . . .
. . . .
. . . .
. . . .
. . . .
. . . .
. . . .
. . . .

SMELL / SCENT

. . . .
. . . .
. . . .
. . . .
. . . .
. . . .

OTHER NOTES

. . . .
. . . .
. . . .
. . . .
. . . .
. . . .

BOURBON	

PRODUCER		DISTILLERY	
TYPE / GRADE		COUNTRY	
ALCOHOL %		REGION	
AGE		STILL TYPE	
PRICE		BOTTLE SIZE	

QUALITY RATING

1	2	3	4	5	6	7	8	9	10

VALUE FOR MONEY

1	2	3	4	5	6	7	8	9	10

COLOR METER

- BLACK
- DARK BROWN
- MAHOGANY
- BRICK
- DARK AMBER
- AMBER
- GOLD
- STRAW
- CLEAR

FLAVOR WHEEL

HEAT / ABM _____ %

BALANCE
FINISH
BODY
ESTERY
SHARP / ACIDIC
ASTRINGENT
ROASTED / WOODY
MOLASSES
SWEET / CANDIED
SPICES
HERBAL / VEGETAL
DRIED FRUIT
CITRUS FRUIT
DARK FRUIT
FRESH FRUIT

FLAVOR NOTES

. . . .
. . . .
. . . .
. . . .
. . . .
. . . .
. . . .
. . . .

SMELL / SCENT

. . . .
. . . .
. . . .
. . . .
. . . .
. . . .

OTHER NOTES

. . . .
. . . .
. . . .
. . . .

BOURBON	

PRODUCER		DISTILLERY	
TYPE / GRADE		COUNTRY	
ALCOHOL %		REGION	
AGE		STILL TYPE	
PRICE		BOTTLE SIZE	

QUALITY RATING

1	2	3	4	5	6	7	8	9	10

VALUE FOR MONEY

1	2	3	4	5	6	7	8	9	10

COLOR METER

BLACK

DARK BROWN

MAHOGANY

BRICK

DARK AMBER

AMBER

GOLD

STRAW

CLEAR

FLAVOR WHEEL

HEAT / ABM _____ %

BALANCE
FINISH
BODY
ESTERY
SHARP / ACIDIC
ASTRINGENT
ROASTED / WOODY
MOLASSES
SWEET / CANDIED
SPICES
HERBAL / VEGETAL
DRIED FRUIT
CITRUS FRUIT
DARK FRUIT
FRESH FRUIT

FLAVOR NOTES

. . . .
. . . .
. . . .
. . . .
. . . .
. . . .
. . . .
. . . .
. . . .
. . . .

SMELL / SCENT

. . . .
. . . .
. . . .
. . . .
. . . .
. . . .

OTHER NOTES

. . . .
. . . .
. . . .
. . . .
. . . .
. . . .

BOURBON	

PRODUCER		DISTILLERY	
TYPE / GRADE		COUNTRY	
ALCOHOL %		REGION	
AGE		STILL TYPE	
PRICE		BOTTLE SIZE	

QUALITY RATING

1	2	3	4	5	6	7	8	9	10

VALUE FOR MONEY

1	2	3	4	5	6	7	8	9	10

COLOR METER

BLACK

DARK BROWN

MAHOGANY

BRICK

DARK AMBER

AMBER

GOLD

STRAW

CLEAR

FLAVOR WHEEL

HEAT / ABM _____ %

BALANCE

FINISH

BODY

ESTERY

SHARP / ACIDIC

ASTRINGENT

ROASTED / WOODY

MOLASSES

SWEET / CANDIED

SPICES

HERBAL / VEGETAL

DRIED FRUIT

CITRUS FRUIT

DARK FRUIT

FRESH FRUIT

FLAVOR NOTES

. . . .
. . . .
. . . .
. . . .
. . . .
. . . .
. . . .
. . . .
. . . .
. . . .

SMELL / SCENT

. . . .
. . . .
. . . .
. . . .
. . . .
. . . .

OTHER NOTES

. . . .
. . . .
. . . .
. . . .
. . . .

BOURBON	

PRODUCER		DISTILLERY	
TYPE / GRADE		COUNTRY	
ALCOHOL %		REGION	
AGE		STILL TYPE	
PRICE		BOTTLE SIZE	

QUALITY RATING

1	2	3	4	5	6	7	8	9	10

VALUE FOR MONEY

1	2	3	4	5	6	7	8	9	10

COLOR METER

- BLACK
- DARK BROWN
- MAHOGANY
- BRICK
- DARK AMBER
- AMBER
- GOLD
- STRAW
- CLEAR

FLAVOR WHEEL

HEAT / ABM _____ %

BALANCE
FINISH
BODY
ESTERY
SHARP / ACIDIC
ASTRINGENT
ROASTED / WOODY
MOLASSES
SWEET / CANDIED
SPICES
HERBAL / VEGETAL
DRIED FRUIT
CITRUS FRUIT
DARK FRUIT
FRESH FRUIT

FLAVOR NOTES

....
....
....
....
....
....
....
....
....
....

SMELL / SCENT

....
....
....
....
....
....
....

OTHER NOTES

....
....
....
....
....
....
....

DATE _____

BOURBON	

PRODUCER		DISTILLERY	
TYPE / GRADE		COUNTRY	
ALCOHOL %		REGION	
AGE		STILL TYPE	
PRICE		BOTTLE SIZE	

QUALITY RATING

1	2	3	4	5	6	7	8	9	10

VALUE FOR MONEY

1	2	3	4	5	6	7	8	9	10

COLOR METER

BLACK

DARK BROWN

MAHOGANY

BRICK

DARK AMBER

AMBER

GOLD

STRAW

CLEAR

FLAVOR WHEEL

BALANCE · HEAT / ABM _____ % · FINISH · BODY · ESTERY · SHARP / ACIDIC · ASTRINGENT · ROASTED / WOODY · MOLASSES · SWEET / CANDIED · SPICES · HERBAL / VEGETAL · DRIED FRUIT · CITRUS FRUIT · DARK FRUIT · FRESH FRUIT

FLAVOR NOTES

....

SMELL / SCENT

....

OTHER NOTES

....

20

BOURBON	

PRODUCER		DISTILLERY	
TYPE / GRADE		COUNTRY	
ALCOHOL %		REGION	
AGE		STILL TYPE	
PRICE		BOTTLE SIZE	

QUALITY RATING

1	2	3	4	5	6	7	8	9	10

VALUE FOR MONEY

1	2	3	4	5	6	7	8	9	10

COLOR METER

BLACK

DARK BROWN

MAHOGANY

BRICK

DARK AMBER

AMBER

GOLD

STRAW

CLEAR

FLAVOR WHEEL

HEAT / ABM _____ %
BALANCE
FINISH
BODY
ESTERY
SHARP / ACIDIC
ASTRINGENT
ROASTED / WOODY
MOLASSES
SWEET / CANDIED
SPICES
HERBAL / VEGETAL
DRIED FRUIT
CITRUS FRUIT
DARK FRUIT
FRESH FRUIT

FLAVOR NOTES

SMELL / SCENT

OTHER NOTES

BOURBON	

PRODUCER		DISTILLERY	
TYPE / GRADE		COUNTRY	
ALCOHOL %		REGION	
AGE		STILL TYPE	
PRICE		BOTTLE SIZE	

QUALITY RATING

1	2	3	4	5	6	7	8	9	10

VALUE FOR MONEY

1	2	3	4	5	6	7	8	9	10

COLOR METER

BLACK

DARK BROWN

MAHOGANY

BRICK

DARK AMBER

AMBER

GOLD

STRAW

CLEAR

FLAVOR WHEEL

BALANCE HEAT / ABM _____ %
FINISH
BODY
ESTERY
SHARP / ACIDIC
ASTRINGENT
ROASTED / WOODY
MOLASSES
SWEET / CANDIED
SPICES
HERBAL / VEGETAL
DRIED FRUIT
CITRUS FRUIT
DARK FRUIT
FRESH FRUIT

FLAVOR NOTES

. . . .
. . . .
. . . .
. . . .
. . . .
. . . .
. . . .
. . . .
. . . .
. . . .

SMELL / SCENT

. . . .
. . . .
. . . .
. . . .
. . . .
. . . .

OTHER NOTES

. . . .
. . . .
. . . .
. . . .
. . . .

BOURBON	

PRODUCER		DISTILLERY	
TYPE / GRADE		COUNTRY	
ALCOHOL %		REGION	
AGE		STILL TYPE	
PRICE		BOTTLE SIZE	

QUALITY RATING

1	2	3	4	5	6	7	8	9	10

VALUE FOR MONEY

1	2	3	4	5	6	7	8	9	10

COLOR METER

BLACK

DARK BROWN

MAHOGANY

BRICK

DARK AMBER

AMBER

GOLD

STRAW

CLEAR

FLAVOR WHEEL

HEAT / ABM _____ %

BALANCE

FINISH

BODY

ESTERY

SHARP / ACIDIC

ASTRINGENT

ROASTED / WOODY

MOLASSES

SWEET / CANDIED

SPICES

HERBAL / VEGETAL

DRIED FRUIT

CITRUS FRUIT

DARK FRUIT

FRESH FRUIT

FLAVOR NOTES

....
....
....
....
....
....
....
....
....
....

SMELL / SCENT

....
....
....
....
....
....

OTHER NOTES

....
....
....
....
....
....

DATE _____

BOURBON	

PRODUCER		DISTILLERY	
TYPE / GRADE		COUNTRY	
ALCOHOL %		REGION	
AGE		STILL TYPE	
PRICE		BOTTLE SIZE	

QUALITY RATING

1	2	3	4	5	6	7	8	9	10

VALUE FOR MONEY

1	2	3	4	5	6	7	8	9	10

COLOR METER

BLACK

DARK BROWN

MAHOGANY

BRICK

DARK AMBER

AMBER

GOLD

STRAW

CLEAR

FLAVOR WHEEL

HEAT / ABM _____ %

BALANCE, FINISH, BODY, ESTERY, SHARP / ACIDIC, ASTRINGENT, ROASTED / WOODY, MOLASSES, SWEET / CANDIED, SPICES, HERBAL / VEGETAL, DRIED FRUIT, CITRUS FRUIT, DARK FRUIT, FRESH FRUIT

FLAVOR NOTES

SMELL / SCENT

OTHER NOTES

DATE _____

BOURBON	

PRODUCER		DISTILLERY	
TYPE / GRADE		COUNTRY	
ALCOHOL %		REGION	
AGE		STILL TYPE	
PRICE		BOTTLE SIZE	

QUALITY RATING

1	2	3	4	5	6	7	8	9	10

VALUE FOR MONEY

1	2	3	4	5	6	7	8	9	10

COLOR METER

BLACK

DARK BROWN

MAHOGANY

BRICK

DARK AMBER

AMBER

GOLD

STRAW

CLEAR

FLAVOR WHEEL

HEAT / ABM _____ %

BALANCE

FINISH

BODY

ESTERY

SHARP / ACIDIC

ASTRINGENT

ROASTED / WOODY

MOLASSES

SWEET / CANDIED

SPICES

HERBAL / VEGETAL

DRIED FRUIT

CITRUS FRUIT

DARK FRUIT

FRESH FRUIT

FLAVOR NOTES

SMELL / SCENT

OTHER NOTES

BOURBON

PRODUCER		DISTILLERY	
TYPE / GRADE		COUNTRY	
ALCOHOL %		REGION	
AGE		STILL TYPE	
PRICE		BOTTLE SIZE	

QUALITY RATING

1	2	3	4	5	6	7	8	9	10

VALUE FOR MONEY

1	2	3	4	5	6	7	8	9	10

COLOR METER

BLACK

DARK BROWN

MAHOGANY

BRICK

DARK AMBER

AMBER

GOLD

STRAW

CLEAR

FLAVOR WHEEL

BALANCE
FINISH
BODY
ESTERY
SHARP / ACIDIC
ASTRINGENT
ROASTED / WOODY
MOLASSES
SWEET / CANDIED
SPICES
HERBAL / VEGETAL
DRIED FRUIT
CITRUS FRUIT
DARK FRUIT
FRESH FRUIT
HEAT / ABM _____ %

FLAVOR NOTES

. . . .
. . . .
. . . .
. . . .
. . . .
. . . .
. . . .
. . . .
. . . .
. . . .

SMELL / SCENT

. . . .
. . . .
. . . .
. . . .
. . . .
. . . .

OTHER NOTES

. . . .
. . . .
. . . .
. . . .
. . . .
. . . .

BOURBON

PRODUCER		DISTILLERY	
TYPE / GRADE		COUNTRY	
ALCOHOL %		REGION	
AGE		STILL TYPE	
PRICE		BOTTLE SIZE	

QUALITY RATING

1	2	3	4	5	6	7	8	9	10

VALUE FOR MONEY

1	2	3	4	5	6	7	8	9	10

COLOR METER

- BLACK
- DARK BROWN
- MAHOGANY
- BRICK
- DARK AMBER
- AMBER
- GOLD
- STRAW
- CLEAR

FLAVOR WHEEL

HEAT / ABM _____ %

BALANCE
FINISH
BODY
ESTERY
SHARP / ACIDIC
ASTRINGENT
ROASTED / WOODY
MOLASSES
SWEET / CANDIED
SPICES
HERBAL / VEGETAL
DRIED FRUIT
CITRUS FRUIT
DARK FRUIT
FRESH FRUIT

FLAVOR NOTES

....
....
....
....
....
....
....
....
....
....

SMELL / SCENT

....
....
....
....
....
....

OTHER NOTES

....
....
....
....
....
....

BOURBON	

PRODUCER		DISTILLERY	
TYPE / GRADE		COUNTRY	
ALCOHOL %		REGION	
AGE		STILL TYPE	
PRICE		BOTTLE SIZE	

QUALITY RATING

1	2	3	4	5	6	7	8	9	10

VALUE FOR MONEY

1	2	3	4	5	6	7	8	9	10

COLOR METER

BLACK

DARK BROWN

MAHOGANY

BRICK

DARK AMBER

AMBER

GOLD

STRAW

CLEAR

FLAVOR WHEEL

BALANCE   HEAT / ABM _____ %

FINISH

BODY   FRESH FRUIT

ESTERY   DARK FRUIT

SHARP / ACIDIC   CITRUS FRUIT

ASTRINGENT   DRIED FRUIT

ROASTED / WOODY   HERBAL / VEGETAL

MOLASSES   SPICES

SWEET / CANDIED

FLAVOR NOTES

....
....
....
....
....
....
....
....
....
....

SMELL / SCENT

....
....
....
....
....
....

OTHER NOTES

....
....
....
....
....
....

BOURBON

PRODUCER		DISTILLERY	
TYPE / GRADE		COUNTRY	
ALCOHOL %		REGION	
AGE		STILL TYPE	
PRICE		BOTTLE SIZE	

QUALITY RATING

1	2	3	4	5	6	7	8	9	10

VALUE FOR MONEY

1	2	3	4	5	6	7	8	9	10

COLOR METER

BLACK

DARK BROWN

MAHOGANY

BRICK

DARK AMBER

AMBER

GOLD

STRAW

CLEAR

FLAVOR WHEEL

BALANCE   HEAT / ABM _____ %

FINISH

BODY

ESTERY

SHARP / ACIDIC

ASTRINGENT

ROASTED / WOODY

MOLASSES

SWEET / CANDIED

SPICES

HERBAL / VEGETAL

DRIED FRUIT

CITRUS FRUIT

DARK FRUIT

FRESH FRUIT

FLAVOR NOTES

....
....
....
....
....
....
....
....
....
....

SMELL / SCENT

....
....
....
....
....
....

OTHER NOTES

....
....
....
....
....
....

BOURBON	

PRODUCER		DISTILLERY	
TYPE / GRADE		COUNTRY	
ALCOHOL %		REGION	
AGE		STILL TYPE	
PRICE		BOTTLE SIZE	

QUALITY RATING

1	2	3	4	5	6	7	8	9	10

VALUE FOR MONEY

1	2	3	4	5	6	7	8	9	10

COLOR METER

- BLACK
- DARK BROWN
- MAHOGANY
- BRICK
- DARK AMBER
- AMBER
- GOLD
- STRAW
- CLEAR

FLAVOR WHEEL

BALANCE HEAT / ABM _____ %
FINISH
BODY
ESTERY
SHARP / ACIDIC
ASTRINGENT
ROASTED / WOODY
MOLASSES
SWEET / CANDIED
SPICES
HERBAL / VEGETAL
DRIED FRUIT
CITRUS FRUIT
DARK FRUIT
FRESH FRUIT

FLAVOR NOTES

....
....
....
....
....
....
....
....
....
....

SMELL / SCENT

....
....
....
....
....
....

OTHER NOTES

....
....
....
....
....
....

BOURBON	

PRODUCER		DISTILLERY	
TYPE / GRADE		COUNTRY	
ALCOHOL %		REGION	
AGE		STILL TYPE	
PRICE		BOTTLE SIZE	

QUALITY RATING

1	2	3	4	5	6	7	8	9	10

VALUE FOR MONEY

1	2	3	4	5	6	7	8	9	10

COLOR METER

- BLACK
- DARK BROWN
- MAHOGANY
- BRICK
- DARK AMBER
- AMBER
- GOLD
- STRAW
- CLEAR

FLAVOR WHEEL

BALANCE — HEAT / ABM _____ %
FINISH
BODY
FRESH FRUIT
ESTERY
DARK FRUIT
SHARP / ACIDIC
CITRUS FRUIT
ASTRINGENT
DRIED FRUIT
ROASTED / WOODY
HERBAL / VEGETAL
MOLASSES
SPICES
SWEET / CANDIED

FLAVOR NOTES

SMELL / SCENT

OTHER NOTES

BOURBON	

PRODUCER		DISTILLERY	
TYPE / GRADE		COUNTRY	
ALCOHOL %		REGION	
AGE		STILL TYPE	
PRICE		BOTTLE SIZE	

QUALITY RATING

1	2	3	4	5	6	7	8	9	10

VALUE FOR MONEY

1	2	3	4	5	6	7	8	9	10

COLOR METER

- BLACK
- DARK BROWN
- MAHOGANY
- BRICK
- DARK AMBER
- AMBER
- GOLD
- STRAW
- CLEAR

FLAVOR WHEEL

HEAT / ABM _____ %

BALANCE
FINISH
BODY
ESTERY
SHARP / ACIDIC
ASTRINGENT
ROASTED / WOODY
MOLASSES
SWEET / CANDIED
SPICES
HERBAL / VEGETAL
DRIED FRUIT
CITRUS FRUIT
DARK FRUIT
FRESH FRUIT

FLAVOR NOTES

. . . .
. . . .
. . . .
. . . .
. . . .
. . . .
. . . .
. . . .
. . . .

SMELL / SCENT

. . . .
. . . .
. . . .
. . . .
. . . .
. . . .

OTHER NOTES

. . . .
. . . .
. . . .
. . . .
. . . .
. . . .

BOURBON	

PRODUCER		**DISTILLERY**	
TYPE / GRADE		**COUNTRY**	
ALCOHOL %		**REGION**	
AGE		**STILL TYPE**	
PRICE		**BOTTLE SIZE**	

QUALITY RATING									
1	2	3	4	5	6	7	8	9	10

VALUE FOR MONEY									
1	2	3	4	5	6	7	8	9	10

COLOR METER

- BLACK
- DARK BROWN
- MAHOGANY
- BRICK
- DARK AMBER
- AMBER
- GOLD
- STRAW
- CLEAR

FLAVOR WHEEL

HEAT / ABM _____ %

BALANCE
FINISH
BODY
ESTERY
SHARP / ACIDIC
ASTRINGENT
ROASTED / WOODY
MOLASSES
SWEET / CANDIED
SPICES
HERBAL / VEGETAL
DRIED FRUIT
CITRUS FRUIT
DARK FRUIT
FRESH FRUIT

FLAVOR NOTES

....
....
....
....
....
....
....
....
....
....

SMELL / SCENT

....
....
....
....
....
....

OTHER NOTES

....
....
....
....
....
....

DATE _____

BOURBON	

PRODUCER		DISTILLERY	
TYPE / GRADE		COUNTRY	
ALCOHOL %		REGION	
AGE		STILL TYPE	
PRICE		BOTTLE SIZE	

QUALITY RATING

1	2	3	4	5	6	7	8	9	10

VALUE FOR MONEY

1	2	3	4	5	6	7	8	9	10

COLOR METER

BLACK

DARK BROWN

MAHOGANY

BRICK

DARK AMBER

AMBER

GOLD

STRAW

CLEAR

FLAVOR WHEEL

HEAT / ABM _____ %
BALANCE
FINISH
BODY
FRESH FRUIT
ESTERY
DARK FRUIT
SHARP / ACIDIC
CITRUS FRUIT
ASTRINGENT
DRIED FRUIT
ROASTED / WOODY
HERBAL / VEGETAL
MOLASSES
SPICES
SWEET / CANDIED

FLAVOR NOTES

....
....
....
....
....
....
....
....
....
....

SMELL / SCENT

....
....
....
....
....
....
....

OTHER NOTES

....
....
....
....
....
....

DATE _____

BOURBON	

PRODUCER		DISTILLERY	
TYPE / GRADE		COUNTRY	
ALCOHOL %		REGION	
AGE		STILL TYPE	
PRICE		BOTTLE SIZE	

QUALITY RATING

1	2	3	4	5	6	7	8	9	10

VALUE FOR MONEY

1	2	3	4	5	6	7	8	9	10

COLOR METER

BLACK

DARK BROWN

MAHOGANY

BRICK

DARK AMBER

AMBER

GOLD

STRAW

CLEAR

FLAVOR WHEEL

BALANCE, HEAT / ABM ____ %, FINISH, BODY, ESTERY, SHARP / ACIDIC, ASTRINGENT, ROASTED / WOODY, MOLASSES, SWEET / CANDIED, SPICES, HERBAL / VEGETAL, DRIED FRUIT, CITRUS FRUIT, DARK FRUIT, FRESH FRUIT

FLAVOR NOTES

SMELL / SCENT

OTHER NOTES

35

BOURBON	

PRODUCER		DISTILLERY	
TYPE / GRADE		COUNTRY	
ALCOHOL %		REGION	
AGE		STILL TYPE	
PRICE		BOTTLE SIZE	

QUALITY RATING

1	2	3	4	5	6	7	8	9	10

VALUE FOR MONEY

1	2	3	4	5	6	7	8	9	10

COLOR METER

BLACK

DARK BROWN

MAHOGANY

BRICK

DARK AMBER

AMBER

GOLD

STRAW

CLEAR

FLAVOR WHEEL

HEAT / ABM _____ %

BALANCE
FINISH
BODY
ESTERY
SHARP / ACIDIC
ASTRINGENT
ROASTED / WOODY
MOLASSES
SWEET / CANDIED
SPICES
HERBAL / VEGETAL
DRIED FRUIT
CITRUS FRUIT
DARK FRUIT
FRESH FRUIT

FLAVOR NOTES

....
....
....
....
....
....
....
....
....
....
....

SMELL / SCENT

....
....
....
....
....
....

OTHER NOTES

....
....
....
....
....
....

BOURBON

PRODUCER		DISTILLERY	
TYPE / GRADE		COUNTRY	
ALCOHOL %		REGION	
AGE		STILL TYPE	
PRICE		BOTTLE SIZE	

QUALITY RATING

1	2	3	4	5	6	7	8	9	10

VALUE FOR MONEY

1	2	3	4	5	6	7	8	9	10

COLOR METER

BLACK

DARK BROWN

MAHOGANY

BRICK

DARK AMBER

AMBER

GOLD

STRAW

CLEAR

FLAVOR WHEEL

HEAT / ABM _____ %

BALANCE
FINISH
BODY
ESTERY
SHARP / ACIDIC
ASTRINGENT
ROASTED / WOODY
MOLASSES
SWEET / CANDIED
SPICES
HERBAL / VEGETAL
DRIED FRUIT
CITRUS FRUIT
DARK FRUIT
FRESH FRUIT

FLAVOR NOTES

SMELL / SCENT

OTHER NOTES

DATE _____

BOURBON	

PRODUCER		DISTILLERY	
TYPE / GRADE		COUNTRY	
ALCOHOL %		REGION	
AGE		STILL TYPE	
PRICE		BOTTLE SIZE	

QUALITY RATING

1	2	3	4	5	6	7	8	9	10

VALUE FOR MONEY

1	2	3	4	5	6	7	8	9	10

COLOR METER

- BLACK
- DARK BROWN
- MAHOGANY
- BRICK
- DARK AMBER
- AMBER
- GOLD
- STRAW
- CLEAR

FLAVOR WHEEL

BALANCE · HEAT / ABM ____ %
FINISH · FRESH FRUIT
BODY · DARK FRUIT
ESTERY · CITRUS FRUIT
SHARP / ACIDIC · DRIED FRUIT
ASTRINGENT · HERBAL / VEGETAL
ROASTED / WOODY · SPICES
MOLASSES · SWEET / CANDIED

FLAVOR NOTES

....
....
....
....
....
....
....
....
....
....
....

SMELL / SCENT

....
....
....
....
....
....

OTHER NOTES

....
....
....
....
....
....

BOURBON	

PRODUCER		DISTILLERY	
TYPE / GRADE		COUNTRY	
ALCOHOL %		REGION	
AGE		STILL TYPE	
PRICE		BOTTLE SIZE	

QUALITY RATING

1	2	3	4	5	6	7	8	9	10

VALUE FOR MONEY

1	2	3	4	5	6	7	8	9	10

COLOR METER

BLACK

DARK BROWN

MAHOGANY

BRICK

DARK AMBER

AMBER

GOLD

STRAW

CLEAR

FLAVOR WHEEL

HEAT / ABM _____ %

BALANCE
FINISH
BODY
ESTERY
SHARP / ACIDIC
ASTRINGENT
ROASTED / WOODY
MOLASSES
SWEET / CANDIED
SPICES
HERBAL / VEGETAL
DRIED FRUIT
CITRUS FRUIT
DARK FRUIT
FRESH FRUIT

FLAVOR NOTES

SMELL / SCENT

OTHER NOTES

39

BOURBON	

PRODUCER		DISTILLERY	
TYPE / GRADE		COUNTRY	
ALCOHOL %		REGION	
AGE		STILL TYPE	
PRICE		BOTTLE SIZE	

QUALITY RATING

1	2	3	4	5	6	7	8	9	10

VALUE FOR MONEY

1	2	3	4	5	6	7	8	9	10

COLOR METER

BLACK

DARK BROWN

MAHOGANY

BRICK

DARK AMBER

AMBER

GOLD

STRAW

CLEAR

FLAVOR WHEEL

BALANCE
HEAT / ABM _____ %
FINISH
BODY
FRESH FRUIT
ESTERY
DARK FRUIT
SHARP / ACIDIC
CITRUS FRUIT
ASTRINGENT
DRIED FRUIT
ROASTED / WOODY
HERBAL / VEGETAL
MOLASSES
SPICES
SWEET / CANDIED

FLAVOR NOTES

. . . .
. . . .
. . . .
. . . .
. . . .
. . . .
. . . .
. . . .
. . . .
. . . .

SMELL / SCENT

. . . .
. . . .
. . . .
. . . .
. . . .
. . . .

OTHER NOTES

. . . .
. . . .
. . . .
. . . .
. . . .

BOURBON	

PRODUCER		DISTILLERY	
TYPE / GRADE		COUNTRY	
ALCOHOL %		REGION	
AGE		STILL TYPE	
PRICE		BOTTLE SIZE	

QUALITY RATING

1	2	3	4	5	6	7	8	9	10

VALUE FOR MONEY

1	2	3	4	5	6	7	8	9	10

COLOR METER

- BLACK
- DARK BROWN
- MAHOGANY
- BRICK
- DARK AMBER
- AMBER
- GOLD
- STRAW
- CLEAR

FLAVOR WHEEL

BALANCE   HEAT / ABM _____ %

FINISH

BODY   FRESH FRUIT

ESTERY   DARK FRUIT

SHARP / ACIDIC   CITRUS FRUIT

ASTRINGENT   DRIED FRUIT

ROASTED / WOODY   HERBAL / VEGETAL

MOLASSES   SPICES

SWEET / CANDIED

FLAVOR NOTES

....
....
....
....
....
....
....
....
....
....

SMELL / SCENT

....
....
....
....
....
....

OTHER NOTES

....
....
....
....
....
....

BOURBON

PRODUCER		**DISTILLERY**	
TYPE / GRADE		**COUNTRY**	
ALCOHOL %		**REGION**	
AGE		**STILL TYPE**	
PRICE		**BOTTLE SIZE**	

QUALITY RATING

1	2	3	4	5	6	7	8	9	10

VALUE FOR MONEY

1	2	3	4	5	6	7	8	9	10

COLOR METER

- BLACK
- DARK BROWN
- MAHOGANY
- BRICK
- DARK AMBER
- AMBER
- GOLD
- STRAW
- CLEAR

FLAVOR WHEEL

BALANCE • HEAT / ABM _____ %
FINISH • FRESH FRUIT
BODY • DARK FRUIT
ESTERY • CITRUS FRUIT
SHARP / ACIDIC • DRIED FRUIT
ASTRINGENT • HERBAL / VEGETAL
ROASTED / WOODY • SPICES
MOLASSES • SWEET / CANDIED

FLAVOR NOTES

....
....
....
....
....
....
....
....
....
....

SMELL / SCENT

....
....
....
....
....
....

OTHER NOTES

....
....
....
....
....
....

DATE _____

BOURBON	

PRODUCER		DISTILLERY	
TYPE / GRADE		COUNTRY	
ALCOHOL %		REGION	
AGE		STILL TYPE	
PRICE		BOTTLE SIZE	

QUALITY RATING

1	2	3	4	5	6	7	8	9	10

VALUE FOR MONEY

1	2	3	4	5	6	7	8	9	10

COLOR METER

BLACK

DARK BROWN

MAHOGANY

BRICK

DARK AMBER

AMBER

GOLD

STRAW

CLEAR

FLAVOR WHEEL

BALANCE   HEAT / ABM _____ %

FINISH

BODY

ESTERY

SHARP / ACIDIC

ASTRINGENT

ROASTED / WOODY

MOLASSES

SWEET / CANDIED

SPICES

HERBAL / VEGETAL

DRIED FRUIT

CITRUS FRUIT

DARK FRUIT

FRESH FRUIT

FLAVOR NOTES

....
....
....
....
....
....
....
....
....
....
....

SMELL / SCENT

....
....
....
....
....
....
....

OTHER NOTES

....
....
....
....
....
....
....

BOURBON	

PRODUCER		DISTILLERY	
TYPE / GRADE		COUNTRY	
ALCOHOL %		REGION	
AGE		STILL TYPE	
PRICE		BOTTLE SIZE	

QUALITY RATING

1	2	3	4	5	6	7	8	9	10

VALUE FOR MONEY

1	2	3	4	5	6	7	8	9	10

COLOR METER

- BLACK
- DARK BROWN
- MAHOGANY
- BRICK
- DARK AMBER
- AMBER
- GOLD
- STRAW
- CLEAR

FLAVOR WHEEL

BALANCE HEAT / ABM _____ %
FINISH
BODY FRESH FRUIT
ESTERY DARK FRUIT
SHARP / ACIDIC CITRUS FRUIT
ASTRINGENT DRIED FRUIT
ROASTED / WOODY HERBAL / VEGETAL
MOLASSES SPICES
SWEET / CANDIED

FLAVOR NOTES

. . . .
. . . .
. . . .
. . . .
. . . .
. . . .
. . . .
. . . .

SMELL / SCENT

. . . .
. . . .
. . . .
. . . .
. . . .
. . . .

OTHER NOTES

. . . .
. . . .
. . . .
. . . .
. . . .
. . . .

DATE _____

BOURBON	

PRODUCER		DISTILLERY	
TYPE / GRADE		COUNTRY	
ALCOHOL %		REGION	
AGE		STILL TYPE	
PRICE		BOTTLE SIZE	

QUALITY RATING

1	2	3	4	5	6	7	8	9	10

VALUE FOR MONEY

1	2	3	4	5	6	7	8	9	10

COLOR METER

BLACK

DARK BROWN

MAHOGANY

BRICK

DARK AMBER

AMBER

GOLD

STRAW

CLEAR

FLAVOR WHEEL

BALANCE · HEAT / ABM ____ % · FINISH · FRESH FRUIT · BODY · DARK FRUIT · ESTERY · CITRUS FRUIT · SHARP / ACIDIC · DRIED FRUIT · ASTRINGENT · HERBAL / VEGETAL · ROASTED / WOODY · SPICES · MOLASSES · SWEET / CANDIED

FLAVOR NOTES

SMELL / SCENT

OTHER NOTES

BOURBON

PRODUCER		DISTILLERY	
TYPE / GRADE		COUNTRY	
ALCOHOL %		REGION	
AGE		STILL TYPE	
PRICE		BOTTLE SIZE	

QUALITY RATING

1	2	3	4	5	6	7	8	9	10

VALUE FOR MONEY

1	2	3	4	5	6	7	8	9	10

COLOR METER

BLACK

DARK BROWN

MAHOGANY

BRICK

DARK AMBER

AMBER

GOLD

STRAW

CLEAR

FLAVOR WHEEL

HEAT / ABM _____ %

BALANCE

FINISH

BODY

ESTERY

SHARP / ACIDIC

ASTRINGENT

ROASTED / WOODY

MOLASSES

SWEET / CANDIED

SPICES

HERBAL / VEGETAL

DRIED FRUIT

CITRUS FRUIT

DARK FRUIT

FRESH FRUIT

FLAVOR NOTES

....
....
....
....
....
....
....
....
....
....

SMELL / SCENT

....
....
....
....
....
....

OTHER NOTES

....
....
....
....
....
....

BOURBON	

PRODUCER		DISTILLERY	
TYPE / GRADE		COUNTRY	
ALCOHOL %		REGION	
AGE		STILL TYPE	
PRICE		BOTTLE SIZE	

QUALITY RATING

1	2	3	4	5	6	7	8	9	10

VALUE FOR MONEY

1	2	3	4	5	6	7	8	9	10

COLOR METER

BLACK

DARK BROWN

MAHOGANY

BRICK

DARK AMBER

AMBER

GOLD

STRAW

CLEAR

FLAVOR WHEEL

HEAT / ABM _____ %

BALANCE
FINISH
BODY
ESTERY
SHARP / ACIDIC
ASTRINGENT
ROASTED / WOODY
MOLASSES
SWEET / CANDIED
SPICES
HERBAL / VEGETAL
DRIED FRUIT
CITRUS FRUIT
DARK FRUIT
FRESH FRUIT

FLAVOR NOTES

....
....
....
....
....
....
....
....
....
....
....

SMELL / SCENT

....
....
....
....
....
....
....

OTHER NOTES

....
....
....
....
....
....
....

BOURBON	

PRODUCER		DISTILLERY	
TYPE / GRADE		COUNTRY	
ALCOHOL %		REGION	
AGE		STILL TYPE	
PRICE		BOTTLE SIZE	

QUALITY RATING

1	2	3	4	5	6	7	8	9	10

VALUE FOR MONEY

1	2	3	4	5	6	7	8	9	10

COLOR METER

- BLACK
- DARK BROWN
- MAHOGANY
- BRICK
- DARK AMBER
- AMBER
- GOLD
- STRAW
- CLEAR

FLAVOR WHEEL

BALANCE HEAT / ABM _____ %
FINISH
BODY FRESH FRUIT
ESTERY DARK FRUIT
SHARP / ACIDIC CITRUS FRUIT
ASTRINGENT DRIED FRUIT
ROASTED / WOODY HERBAL / VEGETAL
MOLASSES SPICES
SWEET / CANDIED

FLAVOR NOTES

....
....
....
....
....
....
....
....
....
....

SMELL / SCENT

....
....
....
....
....
....

OTHER NOTES

....
....
....
....
....
....

BOURBON

PRODUCER		DISTILLERY	
TYPE / GRADE		COUNTRY	
ALCOHOL %		REGION	
AGE		STILL TYPE	
PRICE		BOTTLE SIZE	

QUALITY RATING

1	2	3	4	5	6	7	8	9	10

VALUE FOR MONEY

1	2	3	4	5	6	7	8	9	10

COLOR METER

- BLACK
- DARK BROWN
- MAHOGANY
- BRICK
- DARK AMBER
- AMBER
- GOLD
- STRAW
- CLEAR

FLAVOR WHEEL

BALANCE   HEAT / ABM _____ %

FINISH
BODY
ESTERY
SHARP / ACIDIC
ASTRINGENT
ROASTED / WOODY
MOLASSES
SWEET / CANDIED
SPICES
HERBAL / VEGETAL
DRIED FRUIT
CITRUS FRUIT
DARK FRUIT
FRESH FRUIT

FLAVOR NOTES

....
....
....
....
....
....
....
....
....
....
....

SMELL / SCENT

....
....
....
....
....
....

OTHER NOTES

....
....
....
....
....
....

DATE _____

BOURBON	

PRODUCER		DISTILLERY	
TYPE / GRADE		COUNTRY	
ALCOHOL %		REGION	
AGE		STILL TYPE	
PRICE		BOTTLE SIZE	

QUALITY RATING

1	2	3	4	5	6	7	8	9	10

VALUE FOR MONEY

1	2	3	4	5	6	7	8	9	10

COLOR METER

BLACK

DARK BROWN

MAHOGANY

BRICK

DARK AMBER

AMBER

GOLD

STRAW

CLEAR

FLAVOR WHEEL

HEAT / ABM _____ %
BALANCE, FINISH, BODY, ESTERY, SHARP / ACIDIC, ASTRINGENT, ROASTED / WOODY, MOLASSES, SWEET / CANDIED, SPICES, HERBAL / VEGETAL, DRIED FRUIT, CITRUS FRUIT, DARK FRUIT, FRESH FRUIT

FLAVOR NOTES

SMELL / SCENT

OTHER NOTES

50

BOURBON

PRODUCER		DISTILLERY	
TYPE / GRADE		COUNTRY	
ALCOHOL %		REGION	
AGE		STILL TYPE	
PRICE		BOTTLE SIZE	

QUALITY RATING

1	2	3	4	5	6	7	8	9	10

VALUE FOR MONEY

1	2	3	4	5	6	7	8	9	10

COLOR METER

- BLACK
- DARK BROWN
- MAHOGANY
- BRICK
- DARK AMBER
- AMBER
- GOLD
- STRAW
- CLEAR

FLAVOR WHEEL

HEAT / ABM _____ %

BALANCE
FINISH
BODY
ESTERY
SHARP / ACIDIC
ASTRINGENT
ROASTED / WOODY
MOLASSES
SWEET / CANDIED
SPICES
HERBAL / VEGETAL
DRIED FRUIT
CITRUS FRUIT
DARK FRUIT
FRESH FRUIT

FLAVOR NOTES

SMELL / SCENT

OTHER NOTES

DATE _____

BOURBON	

PRODUCER		DISTILLERY	
TYPE / GRADE		COUNTRY	
ALCOHOL %		REGION	
AGE		STILL TYPE	
PRICE		BOTTLE SIZE	

QUALITY RATING

1	2	3	4	5	6	7	8	9	10

VALUE FOR MONEY

1	2	3	4	5	6	7	8	9	10

COLOR METER

BLACK

DARK BROWN

MAHOGANY

BRICK

DARK AMBER

AMBER

GOLD

STRAW

CLEAR

FLAVOR WHEEL

HEAT / ABM _____ %
BALANCE
FINISH
BODY
ESTERY
SHARP / ACIDIC
ASTRINGENT
ROASTED / WOODY
MOLASSES
SWEET / CANDIED
SPICES
HERBAL / VEGETAL
DRIED FRUIT
CITRUS FRUIT
DARK FRUIT
FRESH FRUIT

FLAVOR NOTES

. . . .
. . . .
. . . .
. . . .
. . . .
. . . .
. . . .
. . . .
. . . .

SMELL / SCENT

. . . .
. . . .
. . . .
. . . .
. . . .
. . . .

OTHER NOTES

. . . .
. . . .
. . . .
. . . .
. . . .

DATE _____

BOURBON	

PRODUCER		DISTILLERY	
TYPE / GRADE		COUNTRY	
ALCOHOL %		REGION	
AGE		STILL TYPE	
PRICE		BOTTLE SIZE	

QUALITY RATING

1	2	3	4	5	6	7	8	9	10

VALUE FOR MONEY

1	2	3	4	5	6	7	8	9	10

COLOR METER

BLACK

DARK BROWN

MAHOGANY

BRICK

DARK AMBER

AMBER

GOLD

STRAW

CLEAR

FLAVOR WHEEL

HEAT / ABM _____ %

BALANCE

FINISH

BODY

FRESH FRUIT

ESTERY

DARK FRUIT

SHARP / ACIDIC

CITRUS FRUIT

ASTRINGENT

DRIED FRUIT

ROASTED / WOODY

HERBAL / VEGETAL

MOLASSES

SPICES

SWEET / CANDIED

FLAVOR NOTES

....
....
....
....
....
....
....
....
....
....
....

SMELL / SCENT

....
....
....
....
....
....
....

OTHER NOTES

....
....
....
....
....
....

BOURBON	

PRODUCER		DISTILLERY	
TYPE / GRADE		COUNTRY	
ALCOHOL %		REGION	
AGE		STILL TYPE	
PRICE		BOTTLE SIZE	

QUALITY RATING

1	2	3	4	5	6	7	8	9	10

VALUE FOR MONEY

1	2	3	4	5	6	7	8	9	10

COLOR METER

BLACK

DARK BROWN

MAHOGANY

BRICK

DARK AMBER

AMBER

GOLD

STRAW

CLEAR

FLAVOR WHEEL

HEAT / ABM _____ %

BALANCE

FINISH

BODY

ESTERY

SHARP / ACIDIC

ASTRINGENT

ROASTED / WOODY

MOLASSES

SWEET / CANDIED

SPICES

HERBAL / VEGETAL

DRIED FRUIT

CITRUS FRUIT

DARK FRUIT

FRESH FRUIT

FLAVOR NOTES

. . . .
. . . .
. . . .
. . . .
. . . .
. . . .
. . . .
. . . .
. . . .
. . . .
. . . .

SMELL / SCENT

. . . .
. . . .
. . . .
. . . .
. . . .
. . . .

OTHER NOTES

. . . .
. . . .
. . . .
. . . .

DATE _____

BOURBON	

PRODUCER		DISTILLERY	
TYPE / GRADE		COUNTRY	
ALCOHOL %		REGION	
AGE		STILL TYPE	
PRICE		BOTTLE SIZE	

QUALITY RATING

1	2	3	4	5	6	7	8	9	10

VALUE FOR MONEY

1	2	3	4	5	6	7	8	9	10

COLOR METER

BLACK

DARK BROWN

MAHOGANY

BRICK

DARK AMBER

AMBER

GOLD

STRAW

CLEAR

FLAVOR WHEEL

HEAT / ABM _____ %

BALANCE
FINISH
BODY
ESTERY
SHARP / ACIDIC
ASTRINGENT
ROASTED / WOODY
MOLASSES
SWEET / CANDIED
SPICES
HERBAL / VEGETAL
DRIED FRUIT
CITRUS FRUIT
DARK FRUIT
FRESH FRUIT

FLAVOR NOTES

....
....
....
....
....
....
....
....
....
....
....

SMELL / SCENT

....
....
....
....
....
....

OTHER NOTES

....
....
....
....
....
....

DATE _____

BOURBON	

PRODUCER		DISTILLERY	
TYPE / GRADE		COUNTRY	
ALCOHOL %		REGION	
AGE		STILL TYPE	
PRICE		BOTTLE SIZE	

QUALITY RATING

1	2	3	4	5	6	7	8	9	10

VALUE FOR MONEY

1	2	3	4	5	6	7	8	9	10

COLOR METER

BLACK

DARK BROWN

MAHOGANY

BRICK

DARK AMBER

AMBER

GOLD

STRAW

CLEAR

FLAVOR WHEEL

BALANCE, FINISH, BODY, ESTERY, SHARP / ACIDIC, ASTRINGENT, ROASTED / WOODY, MOLASSES, SWEET / CANDIED, SPICES, HERBAL / VEGETAL, DRIED FRUIT, CITRUS FRUIT, DARK FRUIT, FRESH FRUIT, HEAT / ABM ____ %

FLAVOR NOTES

....

SMELL / SCENT

....

OTHER NOTES

....

BOURBON

PRODUCER		DISTILLERY	
TYPE / GRADE		COUNTRY	
ALCOHOL %		REGION	
AGE		STILL TYPE	
PRICE		BOTTLE SIZE	

QUALITY RATING

1	2	3	4	5	6	7	8	9	10

VALUE FOR MONEY

1	2	3	4	5	6	7	8	9	10

COLOR METER

- BLACK
- DARK BROWN
- MAHOGANY
- BRICK
- DARK AMBER
- AMBER
- GOLD
- STRAW
- CLEAR

FLAVOR WHEEL

HEAT / ABM _____ %

BALANCE
FINISH
BODY
ESTERY
SHARP / ACIDIC
ASTRINGENT
ROASTED / WOODY
MOLASSES
SWEET / CANDIED
SPICES
HERBAL / VEGETAL
DRIED FRUIT
CITRUS FRUIT
DARK FRUIT
FRESH FRUIT

FLAVOR NOTES

SMELL / SCENT

OTHER NOTES

BOURBON

PRODUCER		DISTILLERY	
TYPE / GRADE		COUNTRY	
ALCOHOL %		REGION	
AGE		STILL TYPE	
PRICE		BOTTLE SIZE	

QUALITY RATING

1	2	3	4	5	6	7	8	9	10

VALUE FOR MONEY

1	2	3	4	5	6	7	8	9	10

COLOR METER

BLACK

DARK BROWN

MAHOGANY

BRICK

DARK AMBER

AMBER

GOLD

STRAW

CLEAR

FLAVOR WHEEL

BALANCE   HEAT / ABM _____ %

FINISH

BODY   FRESH FRUIT

ESTERY   DARK FRUIT

SHARP / ACIDIC   CITRUS FRUIT

ASTRINGENT   DRIED FRUIT

ROASTED / WOODY   HERBAL / VEGETAL

MOLASSES   SPICES

SWEET / CANDIED

FLAVOR NOTES

....
....
....
....
....
....
....
....
....
....

SMELL / SCENT

....
....
....
....
....
....
....

OTHER NOTES

....
....
....
....
....
....
....

DATE _____

BOURBON	

PRODUCER		DISTILLERY	
TYPE / GRADE		COUNTRY	
ALCOHOL %		REGION	
AGE		STILL TYPE	
PRICE		BOTTLE SIZE	

QUALITY RATING

1	2	3	4	5	6	7	8	9	10

VALUE FOR MONEY

1	2	3	4	5	6	7	8	9	10

COLOR METER

BLACK

DARK BROWN

MAHOGANY

BRICK

DARK AMBER

AMBER

GOLD

STRAW

CLEAR

FLAVOR WHEEL

BALANCE
FINISH
BODY
ESTERY
SHARP / ACIDIC
ASTRINGENT
ROASTED / WOODY
MOLASSES
SWEET / CANDIED
SPICES
HERBAL / VEGETAL
DRIED FRUIT
CITRUS FRUIT
DARK FRUIT
FRESH FRUIT
HEAT / ABM _____ %

FLAVOR NOTES

....
....
....
....
....
....
....
....
....
....
....

SMELL / SCENT

....
....
....
....
....
....
....

OTHER NOTES

....
....
....
....
....
....

DATE _____

BOURBON	

PRODUCER		DISTILLERY	
TYPE / GRADE		COUNTRY	
ALCOHOL %		REGION	
AGE		STILL TYPE	
PRICE		BOTTLE SIZE	

QUALITY RATING

1	2	3	4	5	6	7	8	9	10

VALUE FOR MONEY

1	2	3	4	5	6	7	8	9	10

COLOR METER

- BLACK
- DARK BROWN
- MAHOGANY
- BRICK
- DARK AMBER
- AMBER
- GOLD
- STRAW
- CLEAR

FLAVOR WHEEL

HEAT / ABM _____ %

BALANCE, FINISH, BODY, ESTERY, SHARP / ACIDIC, ASTRINGENT, ROASTED / WOODY, MOLASSES, SWEET / CANDIED, SPICES, HERBAL / VEGETAL, DRIED FRUIT, CITRUS FRUIT, DARK FRUIT, FRESH FRUIT

FLAVOR NOTES

SMELL / SCENT

OTHER NOTES

BOURBON	

PRODUCER		DISTILLERY	
TYPE / GRADE		COUNTRY	
ALCOHOL %		REGION	
AGE		STILL TYPE	
PRICE		BOTTLE SIZE	

QUALITY RATING

1	2	3	4	5	6	7	8	9	10

VALUE FOR MONEY

1	2	3	4	5	6	7	8	9	10

COLOR METER

- BLACK
- DARK BROWN
- MAHOGANY
- BRICK
- DARK AMBER
- AMBER
- GOLD
- STRAW
- CLEAR

FLAVOR WHEEL

HEAT / ABM _____ %

BALANCE
FINISH
BODY
ESTERY
SHARP / ACIDIC
ASTRINGENT
ROASTED / WOODY
MOLASSES
SWEET / CANDIED
SPICES
HERBAL / VEGETAL
DRIED FRUIT
CITRUS FRUIT
DARK FRUIT
FRESH FRUIT

FLAVOR NOTES

SMELL / SCENT

OTHER NOTES

BOURBON

PRODUCER		DISTILLERY	
TYPE / GRADE		COUNTRY	
ALCOHOL %		REGION	
AGE		STILL TYPE	
PRICE		BOTTLE SIZE	

QUALITY RATING

1	2	3	4	5	6	7	8	9	10

VALUE FOR MONEY

1	2	3	4	5	6	7	8	9	10

COLOR METER

BLACK

DARK BROWN

MAHOGANY

BRICK

DARK AMBER

AMBER

GOLD

STRAW

CLEAR

FLAVOR WHEEL

BALANCE · HEAT / ABM _____ %
FINISH · FRESH FRUIT
BODY · DARK FRUIT
ESTERY · CITRUS FRUIT
SHARP / ACIDIC · DRIED FRUIT
ASTRINGENT · HERBAL / VEGETAL
ROASTED / WOODY · SPICES
MOLASSES · SWEET / CANDIED

FLAVOR NOTES

SMELL / SCENT

OTHER NOTES

BOURBON

PRODUCER		DISTILLERY	
TYPE / GRADE		COUNTRY	
ALCOHOL %		REGION	
AGE		STILL TYPE	
PRICE		BOTTLE SIZE	

QUALITY RATING

1	2	3	4	5	6	7	8	9	10

VALUE FOR MONEY

1	2	3	4	5	6	7	8	9	10

COLOR METER

BLACK

DARK BROWN

MAHOGANY

BRICK

DARK AMBER

AMBER

GOLD

STRAW

CLEAR

FLAVOR WHEEL

HEAT / ABM _____ %

BALANCE

FINISH

BODY

FRESH FRUIT

ESTERY

DARK FRUIT

SHARP / ACIDIC

CITRUS FRUIT

ASTRINGENT

DRIED FRUIT

ROASTED / WOODY

HERBAL / VEGETAL

MOLASSES

SPICES

SWEET / CANDIED

FLAVOR NOTES

....
....
....
....
....
....
....
....
....

SMELL / SCENT

....
....
....
....
....
....
....

OTHER NOTES

....
....
....
....
....
....
....

BOURBON	

PRODUCER		DISTILLERY	
TYPE / GRADE		COUNTRY	
ALCOHOL %		REGION	
AGE		STILL TYPE	
PRICE		BOTTLE SIZE	

QUALITY RATING

1	2	3	4	5	6	7	8	9	10

VALUE FOR MONEY

1	2	3	4	5	6	7	8	9	10

COLOR METER

BLACK

DARK BROWN

MAHOGANY

BRICK

DARK AMBER

AMBER

GOLD

STRAW

CLEAR

FLAVOR WHEEL

HEAT / ABM _____ %

BALANCE

FINISH

BODY

ESTERY

SHARP / ACIDIC

ASTRINGENT

ROASTED / WOODY

MOLASSES

SWEET / CANDIED

SPICES

HERBAL / VEGETAL

DRIED FRUIT

CITRUS FRUIT

DARK FRUIT

FRESH FRUIT

FLAVOR NOTES

SMELL / SCENT

OTHER NOTES

DATE _____

BOURBON	

PRODUCER		DISTILLERY	
TYPE / GRADE		COUNTRY	
ALCOHOL %		REGION	
AGE		STILL TYPE	
PRICE		BOTTLE SIZE	

QUALITY RATING

1	2	3	4	5	6	7	8	9	10

VALUE FOR MONEY

1	2	3	4	5	6	7	8	9	10

COLOR METER

BLACK

DARK BROWN

MAHOGANY

BRICK

DARK AMBER

AMBER

GOLD

STRAW

CLEAR

FLAVOR WHEEL

HEAT / ABM _____ %
BALANCE
FINISH
FRESH FRUIT
BODY
ESTERY
DARK FRUIT
SHARP / ACIDIC
CITRUS FRUIT
ASTRINGENT
DRIED FRUIT
ROASTED / WOODY
HERBAL / VEGETAL
MOLASSES
SPICES
SWEET / CANDIED

FLAVOR NOTES

SMELL / SCENT

OTHER NOTES

65

BOURBON	

PRODUCER		DISTILLERY	
TYPE / GRADE		COUNTRY	
ALCOHOL %		REGION	
AGE		STILL TYPE	
PRICE		BOTTLE SIZE	

QUALITY RATING

1	2	3	4	5	6	7	8	9	10

VALUE FOR MONEY

1	2	3	4	5	6	7	8	9	10

COLOR METER

BLACK

DARK BROWN

MAHOGANY

BRICK

DARK AMBER

AMBER

GOLD

STRAW

CLEAR

FLAVOR WHEEL

HEAT / ABM _____ %

BALANCE

FINISH

BODY

ESTERY

SHARP / ACIDIC

ASTRINGENT

ROASTED / WOODY

MOLASSES

SWEET / CANDIED

SPICES

HERBAL / VEGETAL

DRIED FRUIT

CITRUS FRUIT

DARK FRUIT

FRESH FRUIT

FLAVOR NOTES

....
....
....
....
....
....
....

SMELL / SCENT

....
....
....
....
....
....

OTHER NOTES

....
....
....
....
....
....

BOURBON	

PRODUCER		DISTILLERY	
TYPE / GRADE		COUNTRY	
ALCOHOL %		REGION	
AGE		STILL TYPE	
PRICE		BOTTLE SIZE	

QUALITY RATING

1	2	3	4	5	6	7	8	9	10

VALUE FOR MONEY

1	2	3	4	5	6	7	8	9	10

COLOR METER

BLACK

DARK BROWN

MAHOGANY

BRICK

DARK AMBER

AMBER

GOLD

STRAW

CLEAR

FLAVOR WHEEL

BALANCE   HEAT / ABM _____ %

FINISH

BODY

ESTERY

SHARP / ACIDIC

ASTRINGENT

ROASTED / WOODY

MOLASSES

SWEET / CANDIED

SPICES

HERBAL / VEGETAL

DRIED FRUIT

CITRUS FRUIT

DARK FRUIT

FRESH FRUIT

FLAVOR NOTES

....
....
....
....
....
....
....
....
....

SMELL / SCENT

....
....
....
....
....
....
....

OTHER NOTES

....
....
....
....
....
....

DATE _____

BOURBON	

PRODUCER		DISTILLERY	
TYPE / GRADE		COUNTRY	
ALCOHOL %		REGION	
AGE		STILL TYPE	
PRICE		BOTTLE SIZE	

QUALITY RATING

1	2	3	4	5	6	7	8	9	10

VALUE FOR MONEY

1	2	3	4	5	6	7	8	9	10

COLOR METER

- BLACK
- DARK BROWN
- MAHOGANY
- BRICK
- DARK AMBER
- AMBER
- GOLD
- STRAW
- CLEAR

FLAVOR WHEEL

HEAT / ABM _____ %

BALANCE
FINISH
BODY
ESTERY
SHARP / ACIDIC
ASTRINGENT
ROASTED / WOODY
MOLASSES
SWEET / CANDIED
SPICES
HERBAL / VEGETAL
DRIED FRUIT
CITRUS FRUIT
DARK FRUIT
FRESH FRUIT

FLAVOR NOTES

....
....
....
....
....
....
....
....
....
....

SMELL / SCENT

....
....
....
....
....
....
....

OTHER NOTES

....
....
....
....
....
....

DATE _____

BOURBON	

PRODUCER		DISTILLERY	
TYPE / GRADE		COUNTRY	
ALCOHOL %		REGION	
AGE		STILL TYPE	
PRICE		BOTTLE SIZE	

QUALITY RATING

1	2	3	4	5	6	7	8	9	10

VALUE FOR MONEY

1	2	3	4	5	6	7	8	9	10

COLOR METER

BLACK

DARK BROWN

MAHOGANY

BRICK

DARK AMBER

AMBER

GOLD

STRAW

CLEAR

FLAVOR WHEEL

HEAT / ABM _____ %

BALANCE
FINISH
BODY
ESTERY
SHARP / ACIDIC
ASTRINGENT
ROASTED / WOODY
MOLASSES
SWEET / CANDIED
SPICES
HERBAL / VEGETAL
DRIED FRUIT
CITRUS FRUIT
DARK FRUIT
FRESH FRUIT

FLAVOR NOTES

....
....
....
....
....
....
....
....
....
....
....

SMELL / SCENT

....
....
....
....
....
....
....

OTHER NOTES

....
....
....
....
....
....
....

BOURBON	

PRODUCER		DISTILLERY	
TYPE / GRADE		COUNTRY	
ALCOHOL %		REGION	
AGE		STILL TYPE	
PRICE		BOTTLE SIZE	

QUALITY RATING

1	2	3	4	5	6	7	8	9	10

VALUE FOR MONEY

1	2	3	4	5	6	7	8	9	10

COLOR METER

BLACK

DARK BROWN

MAHOGANY

BRICK

DARK AMBER

AMBER

GOLD

STRAW

CLEAR

FLAVOR WHEEL

HEAT / ABM _____ %

BALANCE
FINISH
BODY
ESTERY
SHARP / ACIDIC
ASTRINGENT
ROASTED / WOODY
MOLASSES
SWEET / CANDIED
SPICES
HERBAL / VEGETAL
DRIED FRUIT
CITRUS FRUIT
DARK FRUIT
FRESH FRUIT

FLAVOR NOTES

. . . .
. . . .
. . . .
. . . .
. . . .
. . . .
. . . .
. . . .
. . . .
. . . .

SMELL / SCENT

. . . .
. . . .
. . . .
. . . .
. . . .
. . . .

OTHER NOTES

. . . .
. . . .
. . . .
. . . .
. . . .
. . . .

BOURBON	

PRODUCER		DISTILLERY	
TYPE / GRADE		COUNTRY	
ALCOHOL %		REGION	
AGE		STILL TYPE	
PRICE		BOTTLE SIZE	

QUALITY RATING

1	2	3	4	5	6	7	8	9	10

VALUE FOR MONEY

1	2	3	4	5	6	7	8	9	10

COLOR METER

BLACK

DARK BROWN

MAHOGANY

BRICK

DARK AMBER

AMBER

GOLD

STRAW

CLEAR

FLAVOR WHEEL

BALANCE | HEAT / ABM _____ %
FINISH
BODY
ESTERY
SHARP / ACIDIC
ASTRINGENT
ROASTED / WOODY
MOLASSES
SWEET / CANDIED
SPICES
HERBAL / VEGETAL
DRIED FRUIT
CITRUS FRUIT
DARK FRUIT
FRESH FRUIT

FLAVOR NOTES

....
....
....
....
....
....
....
....
....
....

SMELL / SCENT

....
....
....
....
....
....

OTHER NOTES

....
....
....
....
....
....

DATE _____

BOURBON	

PRODUCER		DISTILLERY	
TYPE / GRADE		COUNTRY	
ALCOHOL %		REGION	
AGE		STILL TYPE	
PRICE		BOTTLE SIZE	

QUALITY RATING

1	2	3	4	5	6	7	8	9	10

VALUE FOR MONEY

1	2	3	4	5	6	7	8	9	10

COLOR METER

BLACK

DARK BROWN

MAHOGANY

BRICK

DARK AMBER

AMBER

GOLD

STRAW

CLEAR

FLAVOR WHEEL

HEAT / ABM _____ %

BALANCE
FINISH
BODY
ESTERY
SHARP / ACIDIC
ASTRINGENT
ROASTED / WOODY
MOLASSES
SWEET / CANDIED
SPICES
HERBAL / VEGETAL
DRIED FRUIT
CITRUS FRUIT
DARK FRUIT
FRESH FRUIT

FLAVOR NOTES

....
....
....
....
....
....
....
....
....
....

SMELL / SCENT

....
....
....
....
....
....

OTHER NOTES

....
....
....
....
....
....

DATE _____

BOURBON	

PRODUCER		DISTILLERY	
TYPE / GRADE		COUNTRY	
ALCOHOL %		REGION	
AGE		STILL TYPE	
PRICE		BOTTLE SIZE	

QUALITY RATING

1	2	3	4	5	6	7	8	9	10

VALUE FOR MONEY

1	2	3	4	5	6	7	8	9	10

COLOR METER

BLACK

DARK BROWN

MAHOGANY

BRICK

DARK AMBER

AMBER

GOLD

STRAW

CLEAR

FLAVOR WHEEL

HEAT / ABM _____ %

BALANCE
FINISH
FRESH FRUIT
BODY
ESTERY
DARK FRUIT
SHARP / ACIDIC
CITRUS FRUIT
ASTRINGENT
DRIED FRUIT
ROASTED / WOODY
HERBAL / VEGETAL
MOLASSES
SPICES
SWEET / CANDIED

FLAVOR NOTES

....
....
....
....
....
....
....
....
....
....

SMELL / SCENT

....
....
....
....
....
....
....

OTHER NOTES

....
....
....
....
....
....

DATE _____

BOURBON	

PRODUCER		DISTILLERY	
TYPE / GRADE		COUNTRY	
ALCOHOL %		REGION	
AGE		STILL TYPE	
PRICE		BOTTLE SIZE	

QUALITY RATING

1	2	3	4	5	6	7	8	9	10

VALUE FOR MONEY

1	2	3	4	5	6	7	8	9	10

COLOR METER

BLACK

DARK BROWN

MAHOGANY

BRICK

DARK AMBER

AMBER

GOLD

STRAW

CLEAR

FLAVOR WHEEL

BALANCE HEAT / ABM _____ %
FINISH
BODY
ESTERY
SHARP / ACIDIC
ASTRINGENT
ROASTED / WOODY
MOLASSES
SWEET / CANDIED
SPICES
HERBAL / VEGETAL
DRIED FRUIT
CITRUS FRUIT
DARK FRUIT
FRESH FRUIT

FLAVOR NOTES

SMELL / SCENT

OTHER NOTES

BOURBON

PRODUCER		DISTILLERY	
TYPE / GRADE		COUNTRY	
ALCOHOL %		REGION	
AGE		STILL TYPE	
PRICE		BOTTLE SIZE	

QUALITY RATING

1	2	3	4	5	6	7	8	9	10

VALUE FOR MONEY

1	2	3	4	5	6	7	8	9	10

COLOR METER

BLACK

DARK BROWN

MAHOGANY

BRICK

DARK AMBER

AMBER

GOLD

STRAW

CLEAR

FLAVOR WHEEL

HEAT / ABM _____ %

BALANCE

FINISH

FRESH FRUIT

BODY

ESTERY

DARK FRUIT

SHARP / ACIDIC

CITRUS FRUIT

ASTRINGENT

DRIED FRUIT

ROASTED / WOODY

HERBAL / VEGETAL

MOLASSES

SPICES

SWEET / CANDIED

FLAVOR NOTES

SMELL / SCENT

OTHER NOTES

BOURBON

PRODUCER		DISTILLERY	
TYPE / GRADE		COUNTRY	
ALCOHOL %		REGION	
AGE		STILL TYPE	
PRICE		BOTTLE SIZE	

QUALITY RATING

1	2	3	4	5	6	7	8	9	10

VALUE FOR MONEY

1	2	3	4	5	6	7	8	9	10

COLOR METER

- BLACK
- DARK BROWN
- MAHOGANY
- BRICK
- DARK AMBER
- AMBER
- GOLD
- STRAW
- CLEAR

FLAVOR WHEEL

HEAT / ABM _____ %

BALANCE
FINISH
BODY
ESTERY
SHARP / ACIDIC
ASTRINGENT
ROASTED / WOODY
MOLASSES
SWEET / CANDIED
SPICES
HERBAL / VEGETAL
DRIED FRUIT
CITRUS FRUIT
DARK FRUIT
FRESH FRUIT

FLAVOR NOTES

SMELL / SCENT

OTHER NOTES

DATE _____

BOURBON

PRODUCER		DISTILLERY	
TYPE / GRADE		COUNTRY	
ALCOHOL %		REGION	
AGE		STILL TYPE	
PRICE		BOTTLE SIZE	

QUALITY RATING

1	2	3	4	5	6	7	8	9	10

VALUE FOR MONEY

1	2	3	4	5	6	7	8	9	10

COLOR METER

BLACK

DARK BROWN

MAHOGANY

BRICK

DARK AMBER

AMBER

GOLD

STRAW

CLEAR

FLAVOR WHEEL

HEAT / ABM _____ %

BALANCE
FINISH
BODY
ESTERY
SHARP / ACIDIC
ASTRINGENT
ROASTED / WOODY
MOLASSES
SWEET / CANDIED
SPICES
HERBAL / VEGETAL
DRIED FRUIT
CITRUS FRUIT
DARK FRUIT
FRESH FRUIT

FLAVOR NOTES

....
....
....
....
....
....
....
....
....
....
....

SMELL / SCENT

....
....
....
....
....
....

OTHER NOTES

....
....
....
....
....
....

77

BOURBON	

PRODUCER		DISTILLERY	
TYPE / GRADE		COUNTRY	
ALCOHOL %		REGION	
AGE		STILL TYPE	
PRICE		BOTTLE SIZE	

QUALITY RATING

1	2	3	4	5	6	7	8	9	10

VALUE FOR MONEY

1	2	3	4	5	6	7	8	9	10

COLOR METER

- BLACK
- DARK BROWN
- MAHOGANY
- BRICK
- DARK AMBER
- AMBER
- GOLD
- STRAW
- CLEAR

FLAVOR WHEEL

HEAT / ABM _____ %

BALANCE
FINISH
FRESH FRUIT
BODY
DARK FRUIT
ESTERY
CITRUS FRUIT
SHARP / ACIDIC
DRIED FRUIT
ASTRINGENT
HERBAL / VEGETAL
ROASTED / WOODY
SPICES
MOLASSES
SWEET / CANDIED

FLAVOR NOTES

SMELL / SCENT

OTHER NOTES

BOURBON

PRODUCER		DISTILLERY	
TYPE / GRADE		COUNTRY	
ALCOHOL %		REGION	
AGE		STILL TYPE	
PRICE		BOTTLE SIZE	

QUALITY RATING

1	2	3	4	5	6	7	8	9	10

VALUE FOR MONEY

1	2	3	4	5	6	7	8	9	10

COLOR METER

- BLACK
- DARK BROWN
- MAHOGANY
- BRICK
- DARK AMBER
- AMBER
- GOLD
- STRAW
- CLEAR

FLAVOR WHEEL

HEAT / ABM _____ %

BALANCE
FINISH
BODY
ESTERY
SHARP / ACIDIC
ASTRINGENT
ROASTED / WOODY
MOLASSES
SWEET / CANDIED
SPICES
HERBAL / VEGETAL
DRIED FRUIT
CITRUS FRUIT
DARK FRUIT
FRESH FRUIT

FLAVOR NOTES

....
....
....
....
....
....
....
....
....

SMELL / SCENT

....
....
....
....
....
....

OTHER NOTES

....
....
....
....
....
....

BOURBON	

PRODUCER		DISTILLERY	
TYPE / GRADE		COUNTRY	
ALCOHOL %		REGION	
AGE		STILL TYPE	
PRICE		BOTTLE SIZE	

QUALITY RATING

1	2	3	4	5	6	7	8	9	10

VALUE FOR MONEY

1	2	3	4	5	6	7	8	9	10

COLOR METER

BLACK

DARK BROWN

MAHOGANY

BRICK

DARK AMBER

AMBER

GOLD

STRAW

CLEAR

FLAVOR WHEEL

HEAT / ABM _____ %

BALANCE
FINISH
BODY
ESTERY
SHARP / ACIDIC
ASTRINGENT
ROASTED / WOODY
MOLASSES
SWEET / CANDIED
SPICES
HERBAL / VEGETAL
DRIED FRUIT
CITRUS FRUIT
DARK FRUIT
FRESH FRUIT

FLAVOR NOTES

....
....
....
....
....
....
....
....
....
....
....

SMELL / SCENT

....
....
....
....
....
....

OTHER NOTES

....
....
....
....
....
....

DATE _____

BOURBON	

PRODUCER		DISTILLERY	
TYPE / GRADE		COUNTRY	
ALCOHOL %		REGION	
AGE		STILL TYPE	
PRICE		BOTTLE SIZE	

QUALITY RATING

1	2	3	4	5	6	7	8	9	10

VALUE FOR MONEY

1	2	3	4	5	6	7	8	9	10

COLOR METER

BLACK

DARK BROWN

MAHOGANY

BRICK

DARK AMBER

AMBER

GOLD

STRAW

CLEAR

FLAVOR WHEEL

HEAT / ABM _____ %
BALANCE
FINISH
BODY
ESTERY
SHARP / ACIDIC
ASTRINGENT
ROASTED / WOODY
MOLASSES
SWEET / CANDIED
SPICES
HERBAL / VEGETAL
DRIED FRUIT
CITRUS FRUIT
DARK FRUIT
FRESH FRUIT

FLAVOR NOTES

SMELL / SCENT

OTHER NOTES

BOURBON	

PRODUCER		DISTILLERY	
TYPE / GRADE		COUNTRY	
ALCOHOL %		REGION	
AGE		STILL TYPE	
PRICE		BOTTLE SIZE	

QUALITY RATING

1	2	3	4	5	6	7	8	9	10

VALUE FOR MONEY

1	2	3	4	5	6	7	8	9	10

COLOR METER

BLACK

DARK BROWN

MAHOGANY

BRICK

DARK AMBER

AMBER

GOLD

STRAW

CLEAR

FLAVOR WHEEL

BALANCE
FINISH
BODY
ESTERY
SHARP / ACIDIC
ASTRINGENT
ROASTED / WOODY
MOLASSES
SWEET / CANDIED
SPICES
HERBAL / VEGETAL
DRIED FRUIT
CITRUS FRUIT
DARK FRUIT
FRESH FRUIT
HEAT / ABM _____ %

FLAVOR NOTES

....
....
....
....
....
....
....
....
....

SMELL / SCENT

....
....
....
....
....
....

OTHER NOTES

....
....
....
....
....
....

BOURBON

PRODUCER		DISTILLERY	
TYPE / GRADE		COUNTRY	
ALCOHOL %		REGION	
AGE		STILL TYPE	
PRICE		BOTTLE SIZE	

QUALITY RATING

1	2	3	4	5	6	7	8	9	10

VALUE FOR MONEY

1	2	3	4	5	6	7	8	9	10

COLOR METER

BLACK

DARK BROWN

MAHOGANY

BRICK

DARK AMBER

AMBER

GOLD

STRAW

CLEAR

FLAVOR WHEEL

HEAT / ABM _____ %

BALANCE
FINISH
BODY
ESTERY
SHARP / ACIDIC
ASTRINGENT
ROASTED / WOODY
MOLASSES
SWEET / CANDIED
SPICES
HERBAL / VEGETAL
DRIED FRUIT
CITRUS FRUIT
DARK FRUIT
FRESH FRUIT

FLAVOR NOTES

....
....
....
....
....
....
....
....
....
....
....

SMELL / SCENT

....
....
....
....
....
....
....

OTHER NOTES

....
....
....
....
....

DATE _____

BOURBON	

PRODUCER		DISTILLERY	
TYPE / GRADE		COUNTRY	
ALCOHOL %		REGION	
AGE		STILL TYPE	
PRICE		BOTTLE SIZE	

QUALITY RATING

1	2	3	4	5	6	7	8	9	10

VALUE FOR MONEY

1	2	3	4	5	6	7	8	9	10

COLOR METER

- BLACK
- DARK BROWN
- MAHOGANY
- BRICK
- DARK AMBER
- AMBER
- GOLD
- STRAW
- CLEAR

FLAVOR WHEEL

HEAT / ABM _____ %

BALANCE
FINISH
BODY
ESTERY
SHARP / ACIDIC
ASTRINGENT
ROASTED / WOODY
MOLASSES
SWEET / CANDIED
SPICES
HERBAL / VEGETAL
DRIED FRUIT
CITRUS FRUIT
DARK FRUIT
FRESH FRUIT

FLAVOR NOTES

....
....
....
....
....
....
....
....
....
....

SMELL / SCENT

....
....
....
....
....
....

OTHER NOTES

....
....
....
....
....

BOURBON

PRODUCER		DISTILLERY	
TYPE / GRADE		COUNTRY	
ALCOHOL %		REGION	
AGE		STILL TYPE	
PRICE		BOTTLE SIZE	

QUALITY RATING

1	2	3	4	5	6	7	8	9	10

VALUE FOR MONEY

1	2	3	4	5	6	7	8	9	10

COLOR METER

- BLACK
- DARK BROWN
- MAHOGANY
- BRICK
- DARK AMBER
- AMBER
- GOLD
- STRAW
- CLEAR

FLAVOR WHEEL

HEAT / ABM _____ %

BALANCE
FINISH
BODY
ESTERY
SHARP / ACIDIC
ASTRINGENT
ROASTED / WOODY
MOLASSES
SWEET / CANDIED
SPICES
HERBAL / VEGETAL
DRIED FRUIT
CITRUS FRUIT
DARK FRUIT
FRESH FRUIT

FLAVOR NOTES

SMELL / SCENT

OTHER NOTES

BOURBON

PRODUCER		DISTILLERY	
TYPE / GRADE		COUNTRY	
ALCOHOL %		REGION	
AGE		STILL TYPE	
PRICE		BOTTLE SIZE	

QUALITY RATING

1	2	3	4	5	6	7	8	9	10

VALUE FOR MONEY

1	2	3	4	5	6	7	8	9	10

COLOR METER

BLACK

DARK BROWN

MAHOGANY

BRICK

DARK AMBER

AMBER

GOLD

STRAW

CLEAR

FLAVOR WHEEL

HEAT / ABM _____ %

BALANCE
FINISH
FRESH FRUIT
BODY
DARK FRUIT
ESTERY
CITRUS FRUIT
SHARP / ACIDIC
DRIED FRUIT
ASTRINGENT
HERBAL / VEGETAL
ROASTED / WOODY
SPICES
MOLASSES
SWEET / CANDIED

FLAVOR NOTES

....
....
....
....
....
....
....
....
....
....
....

SMELL / SCENT

....
....
....
....
....
....

OTHER NOTES

....
....
....
....
....
....

BOURBON	

PRODUCER		DISTILLERY	
TYPE / GRADE		COUNTRY	
ALCOHOL %		REGION	
AGE		STILL TYPE	
PRICE		BOTTLE SIZE	

QUALITY RATING

1	2	3	4	5	6	7	8	9	10

VALUE FOR MONEY

1	2	3	4	5	6	7	8	9	10

COLOR METER

BLACK

DARK BROWN

MAHOGANY

BRICK

DARK AMBER

AMBER

GOLD

STRAW

CLEAR

FLAVOR WHEEL

BALANCE
FINISH
BODY
ESTERY
SHARP / ACIDIC
ASTRINGENT
ROASTED / WOODY
MOLASSES
SWEET / CANDIED
SPICES
HERBAL / VEGETAL
DRIED FRUIT
CITRUS FRUIT
DARK FRUIT
FRESH FRUIT
HEAT / ABM _____ %

FLAVOR NOTES

. . . .
. . . .
. . . .
. . . .
. . . .
. . . .
. . . .
. . . .
. . . .

SMELL / SCENT

. . . .
. . . .
. . . .
. . . .
. . . .
. . . .

OTHER NOTES

. . . .
. . . .
. . . .
. . . .
. . . .
. . . .

BOURBON	

PRODUCER		DISTILLERY	
TYPE / GRADE		COUNTRY	
ALCOHOL %		REGION	
AGE		STILL TYPE	
PRICE		BOTTLE SIZE	

QUALITY RATING

1	2	3	4	5	6	7	8	9	10

VALUE FOR MONEY

1	2	3	4	5	6	7	8	9	10

COLOR METER

BLACK

DARK BROWN

MAHOGANY

BRICK

DARK AMBER

AMBER

GOLD

STRAW

CLEAR

FLAVOR WHEEL

HEAT / ABM _____ %

BALANCE
FINISH
BODY
ESTERY
SHARP / ACIDIC
ASTRINGENT
ROASTED / WOODY
MOLASSES
SWEET / CANDIED
SPICES
HERBAL / VEGETAL
DRIED FRUIT
CITRUS FRUIT
DARK FRUIT
FRESH FRUIT

FLAVOR NOTES

....
....
....
....
....
....
....
....
....
....
....

SMELL / SCENT

....
....
....
....
....
....

OTHER NOTES

....
....
....
....
....

BOURBON

PRODUCER		DISTILLERY	
TYPE / GRADE		COUNTRY	
ALCOHOL %		REGION	
AGE		STILL TYPE	
PRICE		BOTTLE SIZE	

QUALITY RATING

1	2	3	4	5	6	7	8	9	10

VALUE FOR MONEY

1	2	3	4	5	6	7	8	9	10

COLOR METER

BLACK

DARK BROWN

MAHOGANY

BRICK

DARK AMBER

AMBER

GOLD

STRAW

CLEAR

FLAVOR WHEEL

HEAT / ABM _____ %

BALANCE

FINISH

BODY

ESTERY

SHARP / ACIDIC

ASTRINGENT

ROASTED / WOODY

MOLASSES

SWEET / CANDIED

SPICES

HERBAL / VEGETAL

DRIED FRUIT

CITRUS FRUIT

DARK FRUIT

FRESH FRUIT

FLAVOR NOTES

. . . .
. . . .
. . . .
. . . .
. . . .
. . . .
. . . .
. . . .
. . . .

SMELL / SCENT

. . . .
. . . .
. . . .
. . . .
. . . .
. . . .
. . . .

OTHER NOTES

. . . .
. . . .
. . . .
. . . .
. . . .
. . . .
. . . .

BOURBON	

PRODUCER		DISTILLERY	
TYPE / GRADE		COUNTRY	
ALCOHOL %		REGION	
AGE		STILL TYPE	
PRICE		BOTTLE SIZE	

QUALITY RATING

1	2	3	4	5	6	7	8	9	10

VALUE FOR MONEY

1	2	3	4	5	6	7	8	9	10

COLOR METER

BLACK

DARK BROWN

MAHOGANY

BRICK

DARK AMBER

AMBER

GOLD

STRAW

CLEAR

FLAVOR WHEEL

HEAT / ABM _____ %

BALANCE

FINISH

BODY

ESTERY

SHARP / ACIDIC

ASTRINGENT

ROASTED / WOODY

MOLASSES

SWEET / CANDIED

SPICES

HERBAL / VEGETAL

DRIED FRUIT

CITRUS FRUIT

DARK FRUIT

FRESH FRUIT

FLAVOR NOTES

....
....
....
....
....
....
....
....
....

SMELL / SCENT

....
....
....
....
....
....

OTHER NOTES

....
....
....
....
....

BOURBON	

PRODUCER		DISTILLERY	
TYPE / GRADE		COUNTRY	
ALCOHOL %		REGION	
AGE		STILL TYPE	
PRICE		BOTTLE SIZE	

QUALITY RATING

1	2	3	4	5	6	7	8	9	10

VALUE FOR MONEY

1	2	3	4	5	6	7	8	9	10

COLOR METER

BLACK

DARK BROWN

MAHOGANY

BRICK

DARK AMBER

AMBER

GOLD

STRAW

CLEAR

FLAVOR WHEEL

BALANCE HEAT / ABM _____ %

FINISH

BODY

ESTERY

SHARP / ACIDIC

ASTRINGENT

ROASTED / WOODY

MOLASSES

SWEET / CANDIED

SPICES

HERBAL / VEGETAL

DRIED FRUIT

CITRUS FRUIT

DARK FRUIT

FRESH FRUIT

FLAVOR NOTES

SMELL / SCENT

OTHER NOTES

DATE _____

BOURBON	

PRODUCER		DISTILLERY	
TYPE / GRADE		COUNTRY	
ALCOHOL %		REGION	
AGE		STILL TYPE	
PRICE		BOTTLE SIZE	

QUALITY RATING

1	2	3	4	5	6	7	8	9	10

VALUE FOR MONEY

1	2	3	4	5	6	7	8	9	10

COLOR METER

BLACK

DARK BROWN

MAHOGANY

BRICK

DARK AMBER

AMBER

GOLD

STRAW

CLEAR

FLAVOR WHEEL

HEAT / ABM _____ %

BALANCE
FINISH
BODY
ESTERY
SHARP / ACIDIC
ASTRINGENT
ROASTED / WOODY
MOLASSES
SWEET / CANDIED
SPICES
HERBAL / VEGETAL
DRIED FRUIT
CITRUS FRUIT
DARK FRUIT
FRESH FRUIT

FLAVOR NOTES

....
....
....
....
....
....
....
....
....

SMELL / SCENT

....
....
....
....
....
....

OTHER NOTES

....
....
....
....
....

DATE _____

BOURBON	

PRODUCER		DISTILLERY	
TYPE / GRADE		COUNTRY	
ALCOHOL %		REGION	
AGE		STILL TYPE	
PRICE		BOTTLE SIZE	

QUALITY RATING

1	2	3	4	5	6	7	8	9	10

VALUE FOR MONEY

1	2	3	4	5	6	7	8	9	10

COLOR METER

BLACK

DARK BROWN

MAHOGANY

BRICK

DARK AMBER

AMBER

GOLD

STRAW

CLEAR

FLAVOR WHEEL

BALANCE
HEAT / ABM _____ %
FINISH
FRESH FRUIT
BODY
ESTERY
DARK FRUIT
SHARP / ACIDIC
CITRUS FRUIT
ASTRINGENT
DRIED FRUIT
ROASTED / WOODY
HERBAL / VEGETAL
MOLASSES
SPICES
SWEET / CANDIED

FLAVOR NOTES

....
....
....
....
....
....
....
....
....
....
....

SMELL / SCENT

....
....
....
....
....
....
....

OTHER NOTES

....
....
....
....
....
....
....

DATE _____

BOURBON	

PRODUCER		DISTILLERY	
TYPE / GRADE		COUNTRY	
ALCOHOL %		REGION	
AGE		STILL TYPE	
PRICE		BOTTLE SIZE	

QUALITY RATING

1	2	3	4	5	6	7	8	9	10

VALUE FOR MONEY

1	2	3	4	5	6	7	8	9	10

COLOR METER

BLACK

DARK BROWN

MAHOGANY

BRICK

DARK AMBER

AMBER

GOLD

STRAW

CLEAR

FLAVOR WHEEL

HEAT / ABM _____ %

BALANCE
FINISH
BODY
ESTERY
SHARP / ACIDIC
ASTRINGENT
ROASTED / WOODY
MOLASSES
SWEET / CANDIED
SPICES
HERBAL / VEGETAL
DRIED FRUIT
CITRUS FRUIT
DARK FRUIT
FRESH FRUIT

FLAVOR NOTES

....
....
....
....
....
....
....
....
....
....

SMELL / SCENT

....
....
....
....
....
....

OTHER NOTES

....
....
....
....
....
....

BOURBON	

PRODUCER		DISTILLERY	
TYPE / GRADE		COUNTRY	
ALCOHOL %		REGION	
AGE		STILL TYPE	
PRICE		BOTTLE SIZE	

QUALITY RATING

1	2	3	4	5	6	7	8	9	10

VALUE FOR MONEY

1	2	3	4	5	6	7	8	9	10

COLOR METER

BLACK

DARK BROWN

MAHOGANY

BRICK

DARK AMBER

AMBER

GOLD

STRAW

CLEAR

FLAVOR WHEEL

HEAT / ABM _____ %

BALANCE

FINISH

BODY

FRESH FRUIT

ESTERY

DARK FRUIT

SHARP / ACIDIC

CITRUS FRUIT

ASTRINGENT

DRIED FRUIT

ROASTED / WOODY

HERBAL / VEGETAL

MOLASSES

SPICES

SWEET / CANDIED

FLAVOR NOTES

. . . .
. . . .
. . . .
. . . .
. . . .
. . . .
. . . .
. . . .
. . . .

SMELL / SCENT

. . . .
. . . .
. . . .
. . . .
. . . .
. . . .
. . . .

OTHER NOTES

. . . .
. . . .
. . . .
. . . .
. . . .
. . . .
. . . .

DATE _____

BOURBON	

PRODUCER		DISTILLERY	
TYPE / GRADE		COUNTRY	
ALCOHOL %		REGION	
AGE		STILL TYPE	
PRICE		BOTTLE SIZE	

QUALITY RATING

1	2	3	4	5	6	7	8	9	10

VALUE FOR MONEY

1	2	3	4	5	6	7	8	9	10

COLOR METER

BLACK

DARK BROWN

MAHOGANY

BRICK

DARK AMBER

AMBER

GOLD

STRAW

CLEAR

FLAVOR WHEEL

HEAT / ABM _____ %

BALANCE
FINISH
BODY
ESTERY
SHARP / ACIDIC
ASTRINGENT
ROASTED / WOODY
MOLASSES
SWEET / CANDIED
SPICES
HERBAL / VEGETAL
DRIED FRUIT
CITRUS FRUIT
DARK FRUIT
FRESH FRUIT

FLAVOR NOTES

....
....
....
....
....
....
....
....
....
....

SMELL / SCENT

....
....
....
....
....
....

OTHER NOTES

....
....
....
....
....
....

BOURBON	

PRODUCER		DISTILLERY	
TYPE / GRADE		COUNTRY	
ALCOHOL %		REGION	
AGE		STILL TYPE	
PRICE		BOTTLE SIZE	

QUALITY RATING

1	2	3	4	5	6	7	8	9	10

VALUE FOR MONEY

1	2	3	4	5	6	7	8	9	10

COLOR METER

BLACK

DARK BROWN

MAHOGANY

BRICK

DARK AMBER

AMBER

GOLD

STRAW

CLEAR

FLAVOR WHEEL

HEAT / ABM _____ %

BALANCE

FINISH

BODY

ESTERY

SHARP / ACIDIC

ASTRINGENT

ROASTED / WOODY

MOLASSES

SWEET / CANDIED

SPICES

HERBAL / VEGETAL

DRIED FRUIT

CITRUS FRUIT

DARK FRUIT

FRESH FRUIT

FLAVOR NOTES

....
....
....
....
....
....
....
....
....
....
....

SMELL / SCENT

....
....
....
....
....
....

OTHER NOTES

....
....
....
....
....
....

DATE _____

BOURBON	

PRODUCER		DISTILLERY	
TYPE / GRADE		COUNTRY	
ALCOHOL %		REGION	
AGE		STILL TYPE	
PRICE		BOTTLE SIZE	

QUALITY RATING

1	2	3	4	5	6	7	8	9	10

VALUE FOR MONEY

1	2	3	4	5	6	7	8	9	10

COLOR METER

BLACK

DARK BROWN

MAHOGANY

BRICK

DARK AMBER

AMBER

GOLD

STRAW

CLEAR

FLAVOR WHEEL

HEAT / ABM _____ %

BALANCE
FINISH
BODY
ESTERY
SHARP / ACIDIC
ASTRINGENT
ROASTED / WOODY
MOLASSES
SWEET / CANDIED
SPICES
HERBAL / VEGETAL
DRIED FRUIT
CITRUS FRUIT
DARK FRUIT
FRESH FRUIT

FLAVOR NOTES

....
....
....
....
....
....
....
....
....

SMELL / SCENT

....
....
....
....
....
....

OTHER NOTES

....
....
....
....
....
....

BOURBON	

PRODUCER		DISTILLERY	
TYPE / GRADE		COUNTRY	
ALCOHOL %		REGION	
AGE		STILL TYPE	
PRICE		BOTTLE SIZE	

QUALITY RATING

1	2	3	4	5	6	7	8	9	10

VALUE FOR MONEY

1	2	3	4	5	6	7	8	9	10

COLOR METER

BLACK

DARK BROWN

MAHOGANY

BRICK

DARK AMBER

AMBER

GOLD

STRAW

CLEAR

FLAVOR WHEEL

HEAT / ABM _____ %

BALANCE

FINISH

BODY

ESTERY

SHARP / ACIDIC

ASTRINGENT

ROASTED / WOODY

MOLASSES

SWEET / CANDIED

SPICES

HERBAL / VEGETAL

DRIED FRUIT

CITRUS FRUIT

DARK FRUIT

FRESH FRUIT

FLAVOR NOTES

SMELL / SCENT

OTHER NOTES

BOURBON	

PRODUCER		DISTILLERY	
TYPE / GRADE		COUNTRY	
ALCOHOL %		REGION	
AGE		STILL TYPE	
PRICE		BOTTLE SIZE	

QUALITY RATING

1	2	3	4	5	6	7	8	9	10

VALUE FOR MONEY

1	2	3	4	5	6	7	8	9	10

COLOR METER

- BLACK
- DARK BROWN
- MAHOGANY
- BRICK
- DARK AMBER
- AMBER
- GOLD
- STRAW
- CLEAR

FLAVOR WHEEL

HEAT / ABM _____ %

BALANCE
FINISH
BODY
ESTERY
SHARP / ACIDIC
ASTRINGENT
ROASTED / WOODY
MOLASSES
SWEET / CANDIED
SPICES
HERBAL / VEGETAL
DRIED FRUIT
CITRUS FRUIT
DARK FRUIT
FRESH FRUIT

FLAVOR NOTES

....
....
....
....
....
....
....
....
....
....
....

SMELL / SCENT

....
....
....
....
....
....
....

OTHER NOTES

....
....
....
....
....
....

BOURBON	

PRODUCER		DISTILLERY	
TYPE / GRADE		COUNTRY	
ALCOHOL %		REGION	
AGE		STILL TYPE	
PRICE		BOTTLE SIZE	

QUALITY RATING

1	2	3	4	5	6	7	8	9	10

VALUE FOR MONEY

1	2	3	4	5	6	7	8	9	10

COLOR METER

BLACK

DARK BROWN

MAHOGANY

BRICK

DARK AMBER

AMBER

GOLD

STRAW

CLEAR

FLAVOR WHEEL

HEAT / ABM _____ %

BALANCE

FINISH

BODY

FRESH FRUIT

ESTERY

DARK FRUIT

SHARP / ACIDIC

CITRUS FRUIT

ASTRINGENT

DRIED FRUIT

ROASTED / WOODY

HERBAL / VEGETAL

MOLASSES

SPICES

SWEET / CANDIED

FLAVOR NOTES

....
....
....
....
....
....
....
....
....
....

SMELL / SCENT

....
....
....
....
....
....
....

OTHER NOTES

....
....
....
....
....
....

BOURBON

PRODUCER		DISTILLERY	
TYPE / GRADE		COUNTRY	
ALCOHOL %		REGION	
AGE		STILL TYPE	
PRICE		BOTTLE SIZE	

QUALITY RATING

1	2	3	4	5	6	7	8	9	10

VALUE FOR MONEY

1	2	3	4	5	6	7	8	9	10

COLOR METER

- BLACK
- DARK BROWN
- MAHOGANY
- BRICK
- DARK AMBER
- AMBER
- GOLD
- STRAW
- CLEAR

FLAVOR WHEEL

HEAT / ABM _____ %

BALANCE
FINISH
BODY
ESTERY
SHARP / ACIDIC
ASTRINGENT
ROASTED / WOODY
MOLASSES
SWEET / CANDIED
SPICES
HERBAL / VEGETAL
DRIED FRUIT
CITRUS FRUIT
DARK FRUIT
FRESH FRUIT

FLAVOR NOTES

SMELL / SCENT

OTHER NOTES

DATE _____

BOURBON	

PRODUCER		DISTILLERY	
TYPE / GRADE		COUNTRY	
ALCOHOL %		REGION	
AGE		STILL TYPE	
PRICE		BOTTLE SIZE	

QUALITY RATING

1	2	3	4	5	6	7	8	9	10

VALUE FOR MONEY

1	2	3	4	5	6	7	8	9	10

COLOR METER

BLACK

DARK BROWN

MAHOGANY

BRICK

DARK AMBER

AMBER

GOLD

STRAW

CLEAR

FLAVOR WHEEL

HEAT / ABM _____ %
BALANCE
FINISH
BODY
FRESH FRUIT
ESTERY
DARK FRUIT
SHARP / ACIDIC
CITRUS FRUIT
ASTRINGENT
DRIED FRUIT
ROASTED / WOODY
HERBAL / VEGETAL
MOLASSES
SPICES
SWEET / CANDIED

FLAVOR NOTES

SMELL / SCENT

OTHER NOTES

DATE _____

BOURBON	

PRODUCER		DISTILLERY	
TYPE / GRADE		COUNTRY	
ALCOHOL %		REGION	
AGE		STILL TYPE	
PRICE		BOTTLE SIZE	

QUALITY RATING

1	2	3	4	5	6	7	8	9	10

VALUE FOR MONEY

1	2	3	4	5	6	7	8	9	10

COLOR METER

- BLACK
- DARK BROWN
- MAHOGANY
- BRICK
- DARK AMBER
- AMBER
- GOLD
- STRAW
- CLEAR

FLAVOR WHEEL

HEAT / ABM _____ %

BALANCE
FINISH
BODY
ESTERY
SHARP / ACIDIC
ASTRINGENT
ROASTED / WOODY
MOLASSES
SWEET / CANDIED
SPICES
HERBAL / VEGETAL
DRIED FRUIT
CITRUS FRUIT
DARK FRUIT
FRESH FRUIT

FLAVOR NOTES

....
....
....
....
....
....
....
....
....
....

SMELL / SCENT

....
....
....
....
....
....

OTHER NOTES

....
....
....
....
....

DATE _____

BOURBON	

PRODUCER		DISTILLERY	
TYPE / GRADE		COUNTRY	
ALCOHOL %		REGION	
AGE		STILL TYPE	
PRICE		BOTTLE SIZE	

QUALITY RATING

1	2	3	4	5	6	7	8	9	10

VALUE FOR MONEY

1	2	3	4	5	6	7	8	9	10

COLOR METER

- BLACK
- DARK BROWN
- MAHOGANY
- BRICK
- DARK AMBER
- AMBER
- GOLD
- STRAW
- CLEAR

FLAVOR WHEEL

HEAT / ABM _____ %

BALANCE
FINISH
BODY
ESTERY
SHARP / ACIDIC
ASTRINGENT
ROASTED / WOODY
MOLASSES
SWEET / CANDIED
SPICES
HERBAL / VEGETAL
DRIED FRUIT
CITRUS FRUIT
DARK FRUIT
FRESH FRUIT

FLAVOR NOTES

....
....
....
....
....
....
....
....
....

SMELL / SCENT

....
....
....
....
....
....

OTHER NOTES

....
....
....
....
....

Made in the USA
San Bernardino, CA
17 December 2019